taste of home®

almost homemade
2011

taste of home

Editor in Chief: Catherine Cassidy
Vice President, Executive Editor/Books:
Heidi Reuter Lloyd
Food Director: Diane Werner RD
Senior Editor/Books: Mark Hagen
Editors: Krista Lanphier, Michelle Rozumalski
Art Directors: Gretchen Trautman, Edwin Robles, Jr.
Content Production Supervisor: Julie Wagner
Design Layout Artist: Catherine Fletcher
Graphic Design Associate: Juli Schnuck
Proofreaders: Linne Bruskewitz, Julie Schnittka
Recipe Asset System Manager: Coleen Martin
Premedia Supervisor: Scott Berger
Recipe Testing & Editing: Taste of Home Test Kitchen
Food Photography: Taste of Home Photo Studio
Administrative Assistant: Barb Czysz

North American Chief Marketing Officer:
Lisa Karpinski
Vice President/Book Marketing: Dan Fink
Creative Director/Creative Marketing: Jim Palmen

THE READER'S DIGEST ASSOCIATION, INC.
President and Chief Executive Officer:
Mary G. Berner
President, North American Affinities:
Suzanne M. Grimes

International Standard Book Number (10): 0-89821-824-1
International Standard Book Number (13): 978-0-89821-824-4
International Standard Serial Number: 2154-4662

COVER PHOTOGRAPHY
Photographer: Rob Hagen
Food Stylist: Kathryn Conrad
Set Stylist: Melissa Haberman

PICTURED ON FRONT COVER:
Lattice Chicken Potpie, p. 155

PICTURED ON BACK COVER:
Elegant Eggnog Dessert, p. 238
Cherry-Stuffed Pork Chops, p. 120

For other Taste of Home
books and products, visit us at
tasteofhome.com

table of contents

From-Scratch Flavor without the Work!

I get my sausage-and-bean stew started in the slow cooker, then spend the afternoon curled up with a good book. It's an effortless meal that tastes great.

Glenda Holmes • Riley, KS

Today, it's easier than ever for cooks with busy schedules to put a hearty, homemade meal on the dinner table. That's because with Taste of Home Almost Homemade, a deliciously fast supper is only a recipe away!

We've compiled **267** dishes that easily combine from-scratch flavor with the time-saving convenience. How? It's simple! We found and tested recipes that turn convenience products into tasty family dishes that don't tax kitchen time. Best of all, these entrees, soups, desserts and more have all the taste of a from-scratch specialty!

Cut Corners without Sacrificing Style

For time-crunched cooks, it's practical to use off-the-shelf ingredients to add a flavor boost to a recipe or to make preparation easier. Dried soup mixes, prepared spaghetti sauce and roasted red peppers are quick and easy ways to add PIZZAZZ to dishes.

While at the grocery store, pick up ready-made items, such as biscuit mix, boxed rice, frozen phyllo dough or rotisserie chicken, then add just a few ingredients for a dish that's as FAST as takeout but a lot more flavorful!

From savory snacks to out-of-this-world desserts, you'll find a variety of quick family dishes that will ease your cooking load. Your family will be hard-pressed to tell that you used shortcuts to prepare appealing meals, desserts and more. It's the PERFECT solution to your supper-time needs!

Reliable Recipes from a Trusted Source

Every recipe in this beautiful cookbook has been taste-tested and approved by our TEST KITCHEN professionals, so you can be sure that you are serving your family the best. Plus, the recipes come from busy home cooks just like you! You'll also find helpful kitchen tips throughout the book that offer sage cooking advice.

With easy-to-follow directions and wonderful color photographs, Taste of Home Almost Homemade will be your most dog-eared cookbook of the year!

WHAT'S INSIDE

Easy Entertaining

Taste of Home Almost Homemade puts the sanity back into having get-togethers with fast-to-fix party recipes in the chapter "Snacks & Appetizers." These treats are as easy as they are yummy, such as Hot Cheddar Mushroom Spread (page 13), made with canned mushrooms, ranch salad dressing mix and a few other on-hand items. It's ready in moments!

If you're looking to impress guests but you're short on time, see the chapter "Holidays & Parties." That's where you'll surprise family and friends with no-fuss recipes such as Caesar New York Strips (page 220), made with only 3 ingredients, plus salt and pepper!

Rise & Shine

The recipes in the "Breakfast & Brunch" chapter make cooking the first meal of the day a cinch for harried home cooks. Morning favorites, such as Lemon Poppy Seed Waffles (page 40) and elegant Eggs with Feta and Asparagus (page 43) are each prepared and ready to go in only 20 minutes!

Fast Fixings

Finding just the right main-course accompaniments to create a balanced meal can be a challenge, but not with the items offered in the chapters "Standout Side Dishes" and "Bountiful Breads." The recipe for Broiled Tomatoes with Artichokes (page 67) takes a mere 15 minutes to make, and Swirled Dill Rolls (page 97) have a prep time of just 25 minutes!

A warm bowl of comfort is only pages away with the recipes in the "Sensational Soups" section. Whether you need a quick lunch or hearty dinner, the easy-to-fix chill-chasers, such as Ham 'n' Corn Chowder (page 103) and Green Chili Tomato Soup (page 114), can be on the table in 10 minutes!

Speedy Entrees

Everyday dinners don't have to be a chore, because three chapters in Almost Homemade are dedicated to main-course recipes. You're sure to find several dishes that will become part of your lineup.

"Memorable Main Courses" offers robust ideas, such as Chicken a la King (page 131)—ready in just 20 minutes! "All-in-One Dinners" features casseroles like Ravioli with Sausage (page 149), made with frozen ravioli, smoked sausage, jarred sauce plus 3 common items. It's ready in 20 minutes! "Slow Cooker Specialties" contains staples, such as Barbecue Country Ribs (page 167). This dish starts with chili sauce and ketchup, and has a prep time of 15 minutes!

Sweet Treats

A boxed cake mix or ready-to-bake pie crust can shave hours off the preparation time of a decadent dinner finale. "Delectable Desserts" offers dozens of delights that are chock-full of freshly made flavors that come together in a snap. Satisfying your sweet tooth has never been so fun or easy!

For instance, Black Forest Cake (page 211) uses chocolate cake mix and cherry pie filling to create a truly impressive dessert. Or, you may want to try elegant Sorbet Cream Puffs (page 195). It's made with only five ingredients, and it's ready—from beginning to end—in a mere 10 minutes! For busy home cooks like you, you truly can have your cake and eat it too!

These bite-sized morsels are proof that good things come in small packages. Their quick prep leaves you time to spend with family and friends.

snacks & appetizers

parmesan pretzel rods

PREP: 10 MIN. BAKE: 20 MIN. + COOLING

1 cup grated Parmesan cheese
1 teaspoon garlic powder
1 teaspoon dried oregano
1/2 teaspoon cayenne pepper
6 tablespoons butter, cubed
1/4 cup olive oil
1 package (10 ounces) pretzel rods

1 In a small bowl, combine the cheese, garlic powder, oregano and cayenne; set aside. In a small saucepan, heat butter and oil until butter is melted. Coat two-thirds of each pretzel rod with butter mixture, then roll in cheese mixture. Reheat butter mixture if needed.

2 Place in an ungreased 15-in. x 10-in. x 1-in. baking pan. Bake at 275° for 20-25 minutes or until golden brown, turning once. Cool. Store in an airtight container.

YIELD: ABOUT 2-1/2 DOZEN.

terrific tomato tart

PREP: 15 MIN. BAKE: 20 MIN.

12 sheets phyllo dough (14 inches x 9 inches)
2 tablespoons olive oil
2 tablespoons dry bread crumbs
2 tablespoons prepared pesto
3/4 cup crumbled feta cheese, divided
1 medium tomato, cut into 1/4-inch slices
1 large yellow tomato, cut into 1/4-inch slices
1/4 teaspoon pepper
5 to 6 fresh basil leaves, thinly sliced

1 Place one sheet of phyllo dough on a baking sheet lined with parchment paper; brush with 1/2 teaspoon oil and sprinkle with 1/2 teaspoon bread crumbs. (Keep remaining phyllo covered with plastic wrap and a damp towel to prevent it from drying out.) Repeat layers, being careful to brush oil all the way to edges.

2 Fold each side 3/4 in. toward center to form a rim. Spread with pesto and sprinkle with half of the feta cheese. Alternately arrange the red and yellow tomato slices over cheese. Sprinkle with pepper and remaining feta.

3 Bake at 400° for 20-25 minutes or until crust is golden brown and crispy. Cool on a wire rack for 5 minutes. Remove parchment paper before cutting. Garnish with basil.

YIELD: 8 SERVINGS.

seaside prawn kabobs

PREP: 20 MIN. + MARINATING COOK: 10 MIN.

- 1 can (5-1/4 ounces) unsweetened pineapple chunks
- 3/4 cup roasted garlic teriyaki marinade and sauce
- 16 uncooked jumbo shrimp, peeled and deveined
- 1 small sweet red pepper, cut into 1-inch chunks

1 Drain pineapple, reserving 3 tablespoons juice; set pineapple aside. In a small bowl, combine teriyaki sauce and reserved juice; pour 3/4 cup into a large resealable plastic bag. Add shrimp; seal bag and turn to coat. Refrigerate for 20 minutes. Set aside remaining marinade for basting.

2 Drain and discard marinade. On 16 small metal or soaked wooden skewers, alternately thread one shrimp, one pineapple chunk and one red pepper chunk. Broil 3-4 in. from the heat for 4-5 minutes on each side or until shrimp turn pink, basting with reserved marinade.

YIELD: 16 APPETIZERS.

buying shrimp

Shrimp in the shell come in different sizes, such as medium, large, extra large and jumbo. Uncooked shrimp will have shells that are gray, brown, pink or red. Fresh shrimp should have a firm texture with a mild aroma.

Here is a favorite snack of mine that I find addictive. I love to give it as gifts during the holidays in gift-wrapped, covered coffee cans with a plastic bag lining the inside.

Betty Claycomb
Alverton, PA

caramel
crackers 'n' nuts

PREP: 25 MIN. BAKE: 1 HOUR + COOLING

- 2 packages (6.6 ounces each) miniature cheddar cheese fish-shaped crackers
- 1 cup dry roasted peanuts
- 1 cup packed brown sugar
- 1/2 cup butter, cubed
- 1/2 cup light corn syrup
- 1 teaspoon baking soda
- 1 teaspoon vanilla extract

1 In a large greased bowl, combine crackers and peanuts; set aside. In a large heavy saucepan, combine the brown sugar, butter and corn syrup. Cook over medium heat until a candy thermometer reads 280° (soft-crack stage), stirring occasionally.

2 Remove from the heat. Add baking soda and vanilla; stir well. Pour over cracker mixture; quickly stir until evenly coated.

3 Transfer to two greased 15-in. x 10-in. x 1-in. baking pans. Bake at 250° for 1 hour, stirring every 15 minutes. Cool; break apart. Store in airtight containers.

YIELD: ABOUT 3 QUARTS.

EDITOR'S NOTE: We recommend that you test your candy thermometer before each use by bringing water to a boil; the thermometer should read 212°. Adjust your recipe temperature up or down based on your test.

hot cheddar-mushroom spread

PREP/TOTAL TIME: 25 MIN.

2 cups mayonnaise

2 cups (8 ounces) shredded cheddar cheese

2/3 cup grated Parmesan cheese

4 cans (4-1/2 ounces each) sliced mushrooms, drained

1 envelope ranch salad dressing mix

Minced fresh parsley

Assorted crackers

1 In a large bowl, combine the mayonnaise, cheeses, mushrooms and dressing mix. Spread into a greased 9-in. pie plate.

2 Bake, uncovered, at 350° for 20-25 minutes or until the cheese is melted. Sprinkle with parsley. Serve with crackers.

YIELD: 3 CUPS.

minced parsley

Here is a simple trimming tip. No need to use the cutting board! Just place fresh parsley in a small glass container and snip the sprigs with kitchen shears until minced.

pizza fingers

PREP: 30 MIN. BAKE: 15 MIN.

I assemble these homemade pizza rolls ahead of time, refrigerate and brush with butter just before baking. Experiment with the filling ingredients as you like.

Nancy Foust • Stoneboro, PA

1/2 pound hard salami, cubed
1/2 pound process cheese (Velveeta), cubed
1 medium green pepper, cubed
1 can (6 ounces) tomato paste
1 tablespoon dried basil
1 tablespoon dried oregano
2 loaves (20 ounces each) sliced sandwich
  bread, crusts removed
1/2 cup butter, melted

1 In a food processor, combine the salami, cheese and green pepper; cover and process until finely chopped. Stir in the tomato paste, basil and oregano.

2 Flatten the bread with a rolling pin. Spread 1 tablespoon salami mixture over one side of each slice of bread. Roll up tightly; cut in half. Place seam side down on a greased baking sheet. Brush with butter. Bake at 375° for 15-18 minutes or until lightly browned. Serve warm.

YIELD: ABOUT 6 DOZEN.

ricotta puffs

PREP: 20 MIN. BAKE: 15 MIN.

1 package (17-1/4 ounces) frozen puff
  pastry, thawed
1/2 cup ricotta cheese
1/2 cup roasted sweet red peppers, drained
  and chopped
3 tablespoons grated Romano or Parmesan
  cheese, divided
1 tablespoon minced fresh parsley
1 teaspoon dried oregano, crushed
1/2 teaspoon pepper
1 teaspoon whole milk

Roasted red peppers and ricotta cheese give these pastry puffs delicious flavor, while parsley and oregano add a little spark.

Maria Regakis • Somerville, MA

1 Unfold puff pastry; cut each sheet into nine squares. In a small bowl, combine the ricotta cheese, red peppers, 2 tablespoons Romano cheese, parsley, oregano and pepper.

2 Brush pastry edges with milk; place 2 rounded teaspoons of cheese mixture in the center of each square. Fold edges of pastry over filling, forming a rectangle; seal edges with a fork. Cut slits in pastry; brush with milk. Sprinkle with remaining Romano cheese.

3 Place on lightly greased baking sheets. Bake at 400° for 15-20 minutes or until golden brown. Remove to a wire rack. Serve warm. Refrigerate leftovers.

YIELD: 1-1/2 DOZEN.

These crispy pockets of spinach and feta cheese with a hint of oregano look like a lot of work, but after assembling a few, you zip through them.
Mrs. McIntyre
Burns Lake, BC

spinach phyllo triangles

PREP: 30 MIN. BAKE: 15 MIN.

1/2 cup chopped onion

1 garlic clove, minced

1 package (10 ounces) frozen chopped spinach, thawed and squeezed dry

1/2 teaspoon dried oregano

1-1/2 cups (6 ounces) crumbled feta cheese

12 sheets phyllo dough (14 inches x 9 inches)

Butter-flavored cooking spray

1 In a nonstick skillet coated with cooking spray, cook onion until tender. Add garlic; cook 1 minute longer. Stir in spinach and oregano; cook over medium-low heat just until spinach is warmed. Drain. Remove from the heat; stir in feta cheese and set aside.

2 Spray one sheet of phyllo dough with butter-flavored cooking spray. (Keep remaining phyllo covered with plastic wrap and a damp towel to prevent drying.) Fold dough in half lengthwise; spray with butter-flavored cooking spray. Cut dough in half lengthwise, forming two strips.

3 Place 1 tablespoon of spinach mixture on lower corner of each strip. Fold dough over filling, forming a triangle. Continue folding, like a flag, until you come to the end of each strip. Spray with butter-flavored cooking spray, making sure all edges are sprayed and sealed. Repeat with remaining phyllo and filling.

4 Place triangles on a baking sheet coated with cooking spray. Bake at 375° for 15-20 minutes or until golden brown. Remove to a wire rack. Serve warm.

YIELD: 2 DOZEN.

ranch-sausage wonton cups

PREP: 20 MIN. BAKE: 5 MIN./BATCH

32 wonton wrappers
1/2 pound bulk Italian sausage
1/2 pound ground beef
3 cups (12 ounces) shredded Colby-Monterey Jack cheese
1 cup mayonnaise
1/2 cup sour cream
1/2 cup whole milk
2 to 3 teaspoons ranch salad dressing mix
1 can (2-1/4 ounces) sliced ripe olives, drained

1 Press wonton wrappers into muffin cups. Bake at 350° for 5 minutes or until lightly browned.

2 Meanwhile, in a large skillet, cook sausage and beef over medium heat until no longer pink; drain. In a large bowl, combine the cheese, mayonnaise, sour cream, milk, salad dressing mix and meat mixture.

3 Spoon 2 tablespoonfuls into each wonton cup; top with olives. Bake for 5-7 minutes or until heated through. Serve warm. Refrigerate leftovers.

YIELD: 32 APPETIZERS.

curried crab pizza

PREP/TOTAL TIME: 30 MIN.

3/4 cup mayonnaise
2 teaspoons curry powder
1 prebaked 12-inch pizza crust
2 cans (6 ounces each) lump crabmeat, drained
3/4 cup shredded part-skim mozzarella cheese
3/4 cup shredded cheddar cheese

1 In a small bowl, combine the mayonnaise and curry. Spread over crust. Sprinkle with crab and cheeses. Place on a pizza pan or baking sheet. Bake at 350° for 20-25 minutes or until cheese is melted.

YIELD: 8-10 SLICES.

pretzel mustard dip

PREP/TOTAL TIME: 10 MIN. + CHILLING

This dip is the perfect snack for the entire family. One taste is never enough!

Bonnie Capper-Eckstein • Maple Grove, MN

1/4 cup mayonnaise
1/4 cup prepared yellow or Dijon mustard
2 tablespoons finely chopped onion
1 tablespoon ranch salad dressing mix
2-1/4 teaspoons prepared horseradish
Pretzels

1 In a small bowl, combine the mayonnaise, mustard, onion, salad dressing mix and horseradish. Cover and refrigerate for at least 30 minutes. Serve with pretzels.

YIELD: ABOUT 1/2 CUP.

peppy provolone slices

PREP/TOTAL TIME: 30 MIN.

1 loaf (1 pound) frozen bread dough, thawed
8 ounces sliced pepperoni
8 ounces sliced provolone cheese
1 cup sliced jalapeno pepper rings

1 On a greased baking sheet, roll out dough into a 15-in. x 12-in. rectangle. Place half of the pepperoni lengthwise in two rows down center third of rectangle. Top with half of the cheese and peppers. Fold one side of dough over filling. Top with remaining pepperoni, cheese and peppers.

2 Fold remaining dough over filling; pinch edges and ends to seal. Bake at 350° for 20-25 minutes or until golden brown. Slice and serve warm.

YIELD: 4-6 SERVINGS.

EDITOR'S NOTE: When cutting hot peppers, disposable gloves are recommended. Avoid touching your face.

This is a great way to use up leftover chicken. Sometimes, I serve it with fruit salad for a delicious, light meal for up to four people.

Sandra Lee Herr
Stevens, PA

chicken turnovers

PREP/TOTAL TIME: 30 MIN.

1 cup diced cooked chicken breast
1 cup (4 ounces) shredded reduced-fat cheddar cheese
1/4 cup chopped celery
1 tablespoon finely chopped onion
1/4 teaspoon salt
1/4 teaspoon pepper
1 tube (8 ounces) refrigerated reduced-fat crescent rolls

1 In a small bowl, combine the chicken, cheese, celery, onion, salt and pepper. Separate crescent dough into eight triangles; top each with chicken mixture. Fold dough over and seal edges.

2 Place on an ungreased baking sheet. Bake at 375° for 13-17 minutes or until golden brown. Serve warm.

YIELD: 8 SERVINGS.

cheese 'n' ham biscuit drops

PREP: 15 MIN. BAKE: 20 MIN.

Flecked with golden cheddar and ham, these flavorful party puffs disappear in two bites.

Mary Detweiler • Middlefield, OH

4 cups shredded cheddar cheese
3 cups biscuit/baking mix
1-1/2 cups finely chopped fully cooked ham (about 10 ounces)
2/3 cup whole milk
1/2 cup grated Parmesan cheese
2 tablespoons minced fresh parsley
2 teaspoons spicy brown mustard

1 In a large bowl, combine all the ingredients and mix well. Shape into 1-in. balls. Place 1 in. apart on greased baking sheets. Bake at 350° for 20-25 minutes or until lightly browned. Serve warm.

YIELD: 7 DOZEN.

artichoke tartlets

PREP: 20 MIN. BAKE: 25 MIN.

Refrigerated pie pastry gives me a head start when making this wonderful recipe. Serve these bite-size quiches as a special snack or at brunch.

Kelly Williams • Morganville, NJ

2 packages (15 ounces each) refrigerated pie pastry

3 eggs

1-1/2 cups heavy whipping cream

1/2 teaspoon salt

12 pitted ripe olives

2 jars (6-1/2 ounces each) marinated artichoke hearts, drained and chopped

1 cup (4 ounces) shredded Swiss cheese

Coarsely ground pepper

1 Roll each pastry sheet into a 10-in. x 8-in. rectangle. Using a 2-1/2-in. round cookie cutter, cut out 12 circles from each rectangle. Press pastry rounds onto the bottom and up the sides of ungreased miniature muffin cups; set aside.

2 In a small bowl, whisk the eggs, cream and salt. Cut each olive into four slices. Place 1 heaping teaspoonful of artichokes in each prepared cup; top with an olive slice and 1 teaspoon of cheese. Pour egg mixture into cups to within 1/4 in. of the top. Sprinkle with the pepper.

3 Bake at 375° for 22-26 minutes or until a knife inserted near center comes out clean. Serve warm.

YIELD: 4 DOZEN.

These cute appetizers taste scrumptious in their phyllo tart shells. They're perfect for any party.
Cheryl Spiropoulos • Hales Corners, WI

phyllo crab cups

PREP: 15 MIN. BAKE: 20 MIN.

1 package (8 ounces) cream cheese, softened

2 to 3 tablespoons horseradish sauce

3/4 cup chopped imitation crabmeat

1 tablespoon chopped green onion

2 packages (1.9 ounces each) frozen miniature phyllo tart shells

Paprika

1 In a small bowl, beat cream cheese and horseradish until smooth. Stir in crab and onion. Spoon 2-3 teaspoonfuls into each tart shell; sprinkle with paprika. Place on a baking sheet.

2 Bake at 350° for 16-18 minutes or until tops begin to brown.

YIELD: 2-1/2 DOZEN.

low-cost "crab"

Imitation crabmeat, also called surimi, is fish that is shaped, flavored and colored to resemble crab. It is typically made from Alaskan pollock, a lean firm fish with a delicate flavor.

chili ham cups

PREP: 15 MIN. BAKE: 20 MIN.

1 package (3 ounces) cream cheese, softened
1 cup finely chopped fully cooked ham
1 cup (4 ounces) shredded cheddar cheese
1 can (4 ounces) chopped green chilies, drained
1/4 cup sliced ripe olives, drained
1 tube (10.2 ounces) refrigerated biscuits
Salsa and sour cream, optional

1 In a small bowl, combine the cream cheese, ham, cheese, chilies and olives. Separate dough into 10 biscuits; press each biscuit onto the bottom and up the sides of a greased muffin cup. Fill with ham mixture.

2 Bake at 375° for 20-25 minutes or until cheese is melted and crust is golden brown. Let stand for 2 minutes before removing from pan. Serve warm. Garnish with salsa and sour cream if desired.

YIELD: 10 SERVINGS.

reuben appetizers

PREP/TOTAL TIME: 15 MIN.

Each year, I collect appetizer recipes to make for the annual Christmas party we throw for friends and family. These tidbits are a big hit every time.

Pat Bohn • Oregon City, OR

1/2 cup Thousand Island salad dressing
4 plain bagels, split
2 to 3 large dill pickles, sliced lengthwise
1 pound thinly sliced deli corned beef
8 slices Swiss cheese

1 Spread salad dressing on each bagel half. Top with pickle slices, corned beef and cheese. Place on an ungreased baking sheet.

2 Broil 6 in. from the heat for 4-6 minutes or until cheese is melted. Cut each into six wedges; serve immediately.

YIELD: 4 DOZEN.

ranch pizza pinwheels

PREP/TOTAL TIME: 25 MIN.

1 tube (13.8 ounces) refrigerated pizza crust
1/4 cup prepared ranch salad dressing
1/2 cup shredded Colby-Monterey Jack cheese
1/2 cup diced pepperoni
1/4 cup chopped green onions
Pizza sauce, warmed or additional ranch salad dressing, optional

1 On a lightly floured surface, roll pizza dough into a 12-in. x 10-in. rectangle. Spread ranch dressing evenly to within 1/4 in. of edges. Sprinkle with cheese, pepperoni and onions. Roll up jelly-roll style, starting with a long side. Cut into 1-in. slices. Place cut side down on a greased baking sheet.

2 Bake at 425° for 10-13 minutes or until lightly browned. Serve warm with pizza sauce or additional ranch dressing if desired. Refrigerate leftovers.

YIELD: 1 DOZEN.

bean and pineapple salsa

PREP/TOTAL TIME: 15 MIN.

1/2 cup canned black beans, rinsed and drained
1/4 cup unsweetened pineapple tidbits, drained
1/4 cup chopped green pepper
1/4 cup chopped sweet red pepper
2 tablespoons finely chopped sweet onion
2 tablespoons chopped green chilies
1/2 to 1 teaspoon chopped seeded
    jalapeno pepper

1 tablespoon rice vinegar
1-1/2 teaspoons minced fresh cilantro
1/2 teaspoon ground coriander
1/2 teaspoon ground cumin
Tortilla chips

1 In a small bowl, combine the first 11 ingredients. Refrigerate until serving. Serve with tortilla chips.

YIELD: 1-1/4 CUPS.

EDITOR'S NOTE: When cutting hot peppers, disposable gloves are recommended. Avoid touching your face.

My mother gave me this recipe more than 10 years ago. Since then, I've made the lip-smacking wings for all different occasions. I must say, they always disappear very quickly.

Tracy Peters
Corinth, MS

spicy ranch chicken wings

PREP: 20 MIN. + MARINATING BAKE: 40 MIN.

4 pounds whole chicken wings
3/4 cup hot pepper sauce
1/4 cup butter, melted
3 tablespoons cider vinegar
1 envelope ranch salad dressing mix
1/2 teaspoon paprika

1 Cut the chicken wings into three sections; discard wing tip sections. In a gallon-size resealable plastic bag, combine the hot pepper sauce, butter and vinegar. Add chicken wings; seal bag and toss to coat evenly. Refrigerate for 4-8 hours.

2 Place the chicken wings on racks in two greased 15-in. x 10-in. x 1-in. baking pans. Sprinkle with dressing mix and paprika. Bake, uncovered, at 350° for 40-50 minutes or until juices run clear.

YIELD: 4 DOZEN.

EDITOR'S NOTE: Uncooked chicken wing sections (wingettes) may be substituted for whole chicken wings.

mini pizza cups

PREP: 25 MIN. BAKE: 15 MIN.

1 tube (11.3 ounces) refrigerated dinner rolls
1 can (8 ounces) pizza sauce
1/4 cup finely chopped onion
1/3 cup finely chopped green pepper
2 ounces sliced turkey pepperoni, chopped
1 cup (4 ounces) shredded part-skim
  mozzarella cheese

1 Separate dough into eight rolls; cut each into quarters. Press dough onto the bottom and up the sides of miniature muffin cups coated with cooking spray.

2 Spoon pizza sauce into each cup. Sprinkle with onion, green pepper, pepperoni and cheese. Bake at 375° for 15-18 minutes or until crusts are browned and cheese is melted.

YIELD: 32 APPETIZERS.

havarti cheese puff

PREP/TOTAL TIME: 30 MIN.

Guests always think I spent a great deal of time on this appetizer and have a hard time guessing the simple ingredients. Havarti is a nice change from the more common Brie.

Marla Reece • Gainesville, FL

1 package (8 ounces) refrigerated crescent rolls
3 tablespoons honey mustard
1 block (8 ounces) Havarti cheese
Assorted crackers

1 On a large piece of waxed paper, unroll crescent dough. Starting with a short side, fold a third of the dough to the center; repeat with the opposite side. Roll out into a 12-in. x 8-in. rectangle.

2 Spread mustard generously over all sides of cheese; place in center of dough. Fold dough over cheese; pinch seams to seal completely.

3 Place on an ungreased baking sheet. Bake at 375° for 15-20 minutes or until golden brown. Serve warm with crackers.

YIELD: 12-16 SERVINGS.

This light and creamy dip is delightful with fruit, and it can even be used as a fluffy, low-cal frosting.

Kim Marie
VanRheenan
Mendota, IL

orange dip for fruit

PREP/TOTAL TIME: 10 MIN.

1 cup orange juice
1 package (3.4 ounces) instant vanilla pudding mix
1 cup (8 ounces) sour cream
1 carton (8 ounces) frozen whipped topping, thawed
Assorted fresh fruit

1 In a large bowl, whisk orange juice and pudding mix. Whisk in sour cream. Fold in whipped topping. Transfer to a serving bowl; serve with fruit. Refrigerate leftovers.

YIELD: 4-1/2 CUPS.

cheddar crab bites

PREP/TOTAL TIME: 25 MIN.

These are perfect for any occasion, and everyone loves them. They also freeze well, too, so I can store some for later.

Elaine Anderson • New Galilee, PA

1 jar (8 ounces) sharp cheddar cheese spread
1 package (8 ounces) imitation crabmeat, chopped
1/2 cup butter, melted
1 teaspoon Worcestershire sauce
1/8 teaspoon garlic powder
6 English muffins, split

1 In a small bowl, combine the cheese spread, crab, butter, Worcestershire sauce and garlic powder. Spread over muffin halves.

2 Place in two ungreased 15-in. x 10-in. x 1-in. baking pans. Bake at 400° for 10-12 minutes or until golden brown. Cut each muffin half into quarters. Refrigerate leftovers.

YIELD: 4 DOZEN.

cabbage bowl nibbler dip

PREP/TOTAL TIME: 50 MIN.

The kids will have fun helping you create this eye-catching appetizer. Fill the hollowed-out cabbage head with your favorite savory dip.

Janice Grandbois • Dyer, IN

1 small head cabbage
2 cups cubed cheddar cheese
3 small cucumbers, cut into 1/4-inch pieces
1 pound thickly sliced deli turkey, cut into 1/4-inch pieces
1 pint grape tomatoes
Frilled toothpicks
1 carton (8 ounces) sour cream ranch dip

1 To prepare serving bowl, gently peel back outer leaves of cabbage. Cut 1/2 in. from bottom of cabbage so it will sit flat. Cut a 3-in. circle in the top of the cabbage; hollow out a third of the cabbage to form a bowl; set aside.

2 Thread the cheese, cucumbers, turkey and tomatoes onto toothpicks. Insert into cabbage, starting at the bottom. Refrigerate until serving. Just before serving, fill cabbage bowl with dip.

YIELD: 24 SERVINGS.

granola trail mix

PREP/TOTAL TIME: 10 MIN.

1 package (18 ounces) granola without raisins
1 package (15 ounces) raisins
1 package (14 ounces) milk chocolate M&M's
1 can (12 ounces) honey-roasted peanuts

1 In a large bowl, combine all ingredients. Store in an airtight container.

YIELD: ABOUT 3 QUARTS.

broiled shrimp canapes

PREP/TOTAL TIME: 30 MIN.

The crisp toast contrasts nicely with mild-flavored shrimp in these savory appetizers. Save time by assembling the topping the day before.

Jeff Johnston • Janesville, WI

10 slices day-old white bread
1/4 cup butter, melted
1-1/2 teaspoons minced fresh thyme
1/2 pound cooked medium shrimp, peeled, deveined and chopped
1/2 cup shredded Swiss cheese
1/2 cup seasoned bread crumbs
1/3 cup mayonnaise

1 Use a 1-1/2-in. round cutter to cut out four circles from each bread slice. Place on a baking sheet. Mix butter and thyme; brush over bread circles. Bake at 400° for 5 minutes or until lightly browned.

2 Combine the shrimp, Swiss cheese, bread crumbs and mayonnaise (mixture will be dry and crumbly). Place 2 teaspoonfuls on each bread circle; press down gently. Broil 6-8 in. from heat for 2-3 minutes or until hot and bubbly. Serve warm.

YIELD: 40 APPETIZERS.

It seems I'm always entertaining at the last minute. I keep many of the ingredients for this rich pizza on hand so I can make it at a moment's notice.

Alicia Sinner
Zion, Illinois

good grating

Before shredding soft cheeses like mozzarella, put the cheese in the freezer for about 30 minutes. This makes it easier to shred because the cheese doesn't stick to the grater.

fantastic artichoke pizza

PREP/TOTAL TIME: 25 MIN.

1 prebaked 12-inch pizza crust
1 can (14 ounces) water-packed artichoke hearts, rinsed, drained and chopped
1 cup (4 ounces) shredded Parmesan cheese, divided
1 cup (4 ounces) shredded part-skim mozzarella cheese, divided
1 cup mayonnaise
6 garlic cloves, minced
1/2 cup sliced grape tomatoes

1 Place crust on an ungreased 14-in. pizza pan. In a small bowl, combine the artichokes, 3/4 cup of each cheese, mayonnaise and garlic; spread over crust.

2 Top with tomatoes. Sprinkle with remaining cheeses. Bake at 450° for 15-20 minutes or until edges are lightly browned.

YIELD: 16 SLICES.

Effortless recipes are a great reason to get up in the morning and make breakfast. From muffins to omelets, there's something here for everyone!

breakfast & brunch

mediterranean frittata

PREP: 15 MIN. BAKE: 30 MIN.

2 medium onions, halved and thinly sliced

2 tablespoons olive oil

2 garlic cloves, minced

1/2 cup chopped roasted sweet red peppers, drained

1/2 cup chopped pimiento-stuffed olives

3 cups cubed Italian bread

1/2 cup crumbled feta cheese

6 eggs

1/2 cup chicken broth

1/4 teaspoon pepper

1 In a large skillet, saute onions in oil until tender. Add garlic; cook 1 minute longer. Remove from the heat. Stir in red peppers and olives. Place bread cubes in a greased 9-in. deep-dish pie plate. Top with onion mixture and cheese.

2 In a large bowl, whisk the eggs, broth and pepper; pour over cheese. Bake at 375° for 30-35 minutes or until a knife inserted near the center comes out clean. Let stand for 5 minutes before cutting into wedges.

YIELD: 6 SERVINGS.

rhubarb sticky buns

PREP: 25 MIN. + RISING BAKE: 20 MIN.

1 package (16 ounces) hot roll mix
4 tablespoons sugar, divided
1 cup warm water (120° to 130°)
1 egg, lightly beaten
2 tablespoons plus 1/2 cup butter, softened, divided
2 cups sliced fresh or frozen rhubarb
1/2 cup packed brown sugar
1/2 cup light corn syrup
2 teaspoons ground cinnamon

1 In a large bowl, combine the contents of the roll mix and yeast packets with 2 tablespoons sugar. Stir in the water, egg and 2 tablespoons butter to form a soft dough. Turn onto a floured surface. Knead until smooth, about 5 minutes. Cover and let rest for 5 minutes.

2 Meanwhile, in a large saucepan, combine the rhubarb, brown sugar, corn syrup and remaining butter. Bring to a boil; cook and stir for 3 minutes. Pour into an ungreased 13-in. x 9-in. baking dish.

3 On a lightly floured surface, roll dough into a 15-in. x 10-in. rectangle. Combine cinnamon and remaining sugar; sprinkle over dough.

4 Roll up jelly-roll style, starting with a long side; pinch seam to seal. Cut into 12 slices. Place cut side down over rhubarb sauce. Cover and let rise in a warm place until doubled, about 30 minutes.

5 Bake at 375° for 20-25 minutes or until golden brown. Immediately invert onto a serving platter. Serve warm.

YIELD: 1 DOZEN.

An envelope of hollandaise sauce mix turns asparagus, deli turkey and English muffins into a special-occasion brunch. The open-faced sandwiches easily impress.

Glenda Campbell
Kodak, TN

turkey eggs benedict

PREP/TOTAL TIME: 20 MIN.

1/2 envelope hollandaise sauce mix

2 tablespoons butter

1/2 cup water

1 teaspoon white vinegar

2 eggs

2 slices deli turkey

1 English muffin, split and toasted

4 bacon strips, cooked

4 asparagus spears, cooked and drained

1 Prepare the hollandaise sauce with butter and water according to package directions.

2 Place 2-3 in. of water in a large skillet, saucepan, or omelet pan with high sides; add vinegar. Bring to a boil; reduce heat and simmer gently. Break cold eggs, one at a time, into a custard cup or saucer; holding the cup close to the surface of the water, slip each egg into water. Cook, uncovered, until whites are completely set and yolks begin to thicken (but are not hard), about 4 minutes.

3 Place a slice of turkey on each muffin half. With a slotted spoon, lift each egg out of the water; place over turkey. Top with bacon, asparagus and Hollandaise sauce.

YIELD: 2 SERVINGS.

EDITOR'S NOTE: This recipe was tested with McCormick's Hollandaise Sauce Blend (1.25-ounce envelope).

hearty brunch pockets

PREP/TOTAL TIME: 25 MIN.

6 brown-and-serve sausage links, sliced

6 ready-to-serve fully cooked bacon strips, diced

6 eggs

2 tablespoons whole milk

1 teaspoon salt

1/4 teaspoon pepper

1 cup (4 ounces) shredded Colby-Monterey Jack cheese

3 pita breads (6 inches), halved

1 In a nonstick skillet, cook sausage for 2 minutes. Add bacon; cook 4 minutes longer or until sausage is heated through and bacon is crisp. Remove and keep warm.

2 In a small bowl, whisk the eggs, milk, salt and pepper. Pour into the skillet; cook and stir over medium heat until eggs are almost set. Add sausage mixture and cheese. Cook and stir for 2 minutes or until eggs are completely set and cheese is melted. Spoon into pita halves.

YIELD: 6 SERVINGS.

canadian bacon waffles

PREP/TOTAL TIME: 20 MIN.

Our home economists cut prep time for this recipe by relying on a biscuit/baking mix. Canadian bacon in the batter makes these waffles a hearty meal-in-one.

Taste of Home Test Kitchen

2 cups biscuit/baking mix

2 eggs, lightly beaten

1/2 cup canola oil

1 cup club soda

1/2 cup chopped Canadian bacon

1/2 cup shredded cheddar cheese

1 teaspoon minced chives

1 In a small bowl, combine the biscuit mix, eggs and oil. Add club soda and stir until smooth. Gently fold in the bacon, cheese and chives.

2 Bake in a preheated waffle iron according to manufacturer's directions until golden brown.

YIELD: 12 WAFFLES.

biscuits with turkey sausage gravy

PREP/TOTAL TIME: 30 MIN.

1 tube (16.3 ounces) large refrigerated flaky biscuits

1 pound Italian turkey sausage links, casings removed

3 tablespoons butter

3 tablespoons all-purpose flour

1/2 teaspoon ground mustard

1/4 teaspoon salt

1/8 teaspoon pepper

2-1/2 cups whole milk

1 tablespoon Worcestershire sauce

1 Bake biscuits according to package directions. Meanwhile, crumble sausage into a large saucepan; cook over medium heat until no longer pink. Drain and keep warm.

2 In the same saucepan, melt butter. Stir in the flour, mustard, salt and pepper until smooth. Gradually add milk and Worcestershire sauce. Bring to a boil; cook and stir for 2 minutes or until thickened.

3 Stir in sausage; heat through. Place two biscuits on each serving plate; top with gravy.

YIELD: 4 SERVINGS.

cranberry-nut coffee cake

PREP: 15 MIN. BAKE: 20 MIN.

If you need a quick treat that will make a lasting impression, give this yummy coffee cake a try!

Lorraine Darocha • Berkshire, MA

2 cups biscuit/baking mix

2 tablespoons sugar

1 egg

2/3 cup whole milk

1/2 cup chopped pecans or walnuts

1/4 cup packed brown sugar

1/4 teaspoon ground cinnamon

2/3 cup whole-berry cranberry sauce

GLAZE:

1 cup confectioners' sugar

1 tablespoon water

1/2 teaspoon vanilla extract

1 In a large bowl, combine the biscuit mix and sugar. Whisk the egg and milk; add to dry ingredients and mix well. Pour into a greased 9-in. square baking pan.

2 Combine the nuts, brown sugar and cinnamon; sprinkle over batter. Spoon cranberry sauce over the top.

3 Bake at 400° for 20-25 minutes or until a toothpick inserted near the center comes out clean. Combine the glaze ingredients; drizzle over warm coffee cake.

YIELD: 9 SERVINGS.

egg 'n' potato burritos

PREP: 20 MIN. COOK: 25 MIN.

1 cup frozen shredded hash brown potatoes

3 green onions, chopped

1 tablespoon olive oil

8 eggs, lightly beaten

1 can (14-1/2 ounces) diced tomatoes with
   mild green chilies, drained

1/2 teaspoon salt

1/2 teaspoon pepper

6 fat-free flour tortillas (8 inches), warmed

1 cup (4 ounces) shredded reduced-fat
   cheddar cheese

This is my husband's favorite dish. The scrumptious combination with hash browns and eggs adds zip to breakfasts on the fly.
Ann Baker • Texarkana, TX

1 In a large nonstick skillet, cook potatoes and onions in oil over medium heat for 8-10 minutes or until potatoes are tender, stirring occasionally.

2 In a large bowl, combine the eggs, tomatoes, salt and pepper. Pour over potatoes. Reduce heat to medium-low. Cook and stir until eggs are completely set. Remove from the heat.

3 Spoon about 1/2 cup of egg mixture down the center of each tortilla; sprinkle with cheese. Fold sides and ends over filling and roll up.

YIELD: 6 SERVINGS.

blueberry oatmeal pancakes

PREP: 20 MIN. COOK: 5 MIN./BATCH

2 cups all-purpose flour

2 packets (1.51 ounces each) instant maple and brown sugar oatmeal mix

2 tablespoons sugar

2 teaspoons baking powder

1/8 teaspoon salt

2 egg whites

1 egg

1-1/2 cups fat-free milk

1/2 cup reduced-fat sour cream

2 cups fresh or frozen blueberries

BLUEBERRY SYRUP:

1-1/2 cups fresh or frozen blueberries

1/2 cup sugar

1 In a large bowl, combine the first five ingredients. In another bowl, whisk the egg whites, egg, milk and sour cream. Stir into dry ingredients just until moistened. Fold in blueberries.

2 Spoon batter by 1/4 cupfuls onto a hot griddle coated with cooking spray. Turn when bubbles form on top of pancake; cook until the second side is golden brown.

3 In a microwave-safe bowl, combine the syrup ingredients. Microwave, uncovered, on high for 1 minute; stir. Microwave 1-2 minutes longer or until hot and bubbly. Serve warm with pancakes.

YIELD: 14 PANCAKES (1-1/4 CUPS SYRUP).

EDITOR'S NOTE: If using frozen blueberries, do not thaw before adding to batter. This recipe was tested in a 1,100-watt microwave.

A few tubes of crescent rolls make this impressive recipe a snap. I fill the ring with chicken salad and serve warm slices with mustard-flavored mayonnaise.

Rebecca Clark
Warrior, AL

chicken club brunch ring

PREP: 20 MIN. BAKE: 20 MIN.

1/2 cup mayonnaise

1 tablespoon minced fresh parsley

2 teaspoons Dijon mustard

1-1/2 teaspoons finely chopped onion

1-3/4 cups cubed cooked chicken breast (1/2-inch cubes)

2 bacon strips, cooked and crumbled

1 cup (4 ounces) shredded Swiss cheese, divided

2 tubes (8 ounces each) refrigerated crescent rolls

2 plum tomatoes

2 cups shredded lettuce

1 In a large bowl, combine the mayonnaise, parsley, mustard and onion. Stir in the chicken, bacon and 3/4 cup cheese.

2 Unroll crescent dough; separate into 16 triangles. Arrange on an ungreased 12-in. round pizza pan, forming a ring with pointed ends facing outer edge of pan and wide ends overlapping.

3 Spoon chicken mixture over wide ends; fold points over filling and tuck under wide ends (filling will be visible). Chop half of a tomato; set aside. Slice remaining tomatoes; place over filling and tuck into dough.

4 Bake at 375° for 20-25 minutes or until golden brown. Sprinkle with remaining cheese. Let stand for 5 minutes. Place lettuce in center of ring; sprinkle with chopped tomato.

YIELD: 16 SERVINGS.

tomato tidbit

When preparing tomatoes for a recipe, a quick way to core them is to slice off the end and use a grapefruit spoon to easily scoop out the core.

Store-bought French toast sticks are spread with strawberry cream cheese to make this fast breakfast fare. I serve these with a citrus fruit puree instead of regular syrup.

Anna Free
Bradner, OH

jazzed-up french toast sticks

PREP/TOTAL TIME: 25 MIN.

  4 ounces spreadable strawberry cream cheese
  12 French toast sticks
  1 snack-size cup (4 ounces) mixed fruit
  1 tablespoon orange juice
  Sliced fresh strawberries, optional

1 Spread the cream cheese over six French toast sticks, about 1 tablespoon on each; top with the remaining sticks. Place in a greased 9-in. square baking pan. Bake at 400° for 15-17 minutes or until golden brown.

2 Meanwhile, in a blender, combine the mixed fruit and orange juice; cover and process until smooth. Serve with French toast sticks. Garnish with strawberries if desired.

YIELD: 3 SERVINGS.

lemon poppy seed waffles

PREP/TOTAL TIME: 20 MIN.

When spring arrives to your area, these lemony waffles make a refreshing rise-and-shine breakfast.

Taste of Home Test Kitchen

  2 cups biscuit/baking mix
  2 eggs, lightly beaten
  1/2 cup canola oil
  1 cup club soda
  1 tablespoon lemon juice
  1 teaspoon vanilla extract
  2 teaspoons poppy seeds

1 In a large bowl, combine the biscuit mix, eggs and oil. In a small bowl, combine the club soda, lemon juice and vanilla; gradually stir into biscuit mixture until smooth. Gently fold in poppy seeds.

2 Bake in a preheated waffle iron according to manufacturer's directions until golden brown.

YIELD: 12 WAFFLES.

country brunch pie

PREP: 15 MIN. BAKE: 40 MIN. + STANDING

Pastry for single-crust pie (9 inches)

1/2 pound bulk pork sausage

3/4 cup shredded part-skim mozzarella cheese

4 eggs

1 cup half-and-half cream

1 can (4 ounces) mushroom stems and pieces, drained

1/4 cup chopped green pepper

1/4 cup chopped sweet red pepper

2 tablespoons chopped onion

1 Line a 9-in. deep-dish pie plate with pastry. Trim to 1/2 in. beyond edge of plate; flute edges. Line pastry shell with a double thickness of heavy-duty foil. Bake at 400° for 5 minutes. Remove the foil and bake 5 minutes longer.

2 In a small skillet, cook sausage over medium heat until no longer pink; drain. Spoon sausage into crust; sprinkle with cheese. In a small bowl, combine the eggs, cream, mushrooms, peppers and onion; pour over cheese.

3 Bake at 375° for 40-45 minutes or until a knife inserted near the center comes out clean. Let stand for 10 minutes before cutting.

YIELD: 6-8 SERVINGS.

1 In a small nonstick skillet coated with cooking spray, cook mushrooms and onion over medium heat until tender. Add the egg substitute and tomato; cook and stir until set.

2 Place one tortilla in a large nonstick skillet; top with ham, egg mixture, cheeses and remaining tortilla. Cook over medium heat, carefully turning once, until lightly browned on both sides and cheese is melted. Cut into four wedges. Serve with salsa.

YIELD: 2 SERVINGS.

cinnamon cherry rolls

PREP: 20 MIN. BAKE: 15 MIN.

These pretty pastries are so elegant that your guests will think you fussed all morning.

Patricia Quinn • Omaha, NE

1/4 cup packed brown sugar

1 teaspoon ground cinnamon

1 tube (8 ounces) refrigerated crescent rolls

2 tablespoons butter, melted, divided

1 jar (10 ounces) maraschino cherries, drained and chopped

3/4 cup confectioners' sugar

4 to 5 teaspoons whole milk

1 In a small bowl, combine the brown sugar and cinnamon; set aside. Unroll crescent dough and separate into triangles. Brush with 1 tablespoon butter. Sprinkle with 1-1/2 teaspoons brown sugar mixture; top with cherries.

2 Roll up from the wide end. Place point side down on a greased baking sheet; curve ends slightly. Brush with remaining butter; sprinkle with remaining brown sugar mixture.

3 Bake at 375° for 12-15 minutes or until golden brown. In a small bowl, combine the confectioners' sugar and enough milk to achieve drizzling consistency; drizzle over warm rolls.

YIELD: 8 ROLLS.

I came up with these crispy quesadillas because my family found breakfast burritos too messy. They're fast to fix, fun to eat, filling and healthy. You can add or subtract ingredients to fit individual tastes.

Terri Capps • Wichita, KS

omelet quesadilla

PREP/TOTAL TIME: 15 MIN.

1 cup sliced fresh mushrooms

2 tablespoons chopped onion

1/2 cup egg substitute

2 tablespoons chopped fresh tomato

2 flour tortillas (10 inches)

4 thin slices lean ham (1/2 ounce each)

1/4 cup shredded part-skim mozzarella cheese

1/4 cup shredded reduced-fat cheddar cheese

3 tablespoons salsa

We always have more than enough asparagus for the two of us, so I whipped up this dish. Now it's become a staple at our breakfast table. I share extra asparagus with my family and friends along with this recipe.

Carol Heine
New Prague, MN

eggs with feta and asparagus

PREP/TOTAL TIME: 20 MIN.

1 cup cut fresh asparagus (2-inch pieces)

1 tablespoon butter

4 eggs

1/8 to 1/4 teaspoon seasoned salt

4 strips ready-to-serve fully cooked bacon, crumbled

1/4 cup crumbled feta cheese

1 Place 1 in. of water in a saucepan; add asparagus. Bring to a boil. Reduce heat; cover and simmer for 3-5 minutes or until crisp-tender.

2 Meanwhile, in a large skillet, heat butter until hot. Add eggs; reduce heat to low. Cook until whites are completely set and yolks begin to thicken but are not hard. Sprinkle with seasoned salt.

3 Transfer eggs to serving plates; top with asparagus, bacon and cheese.

YIELD: 2 SERVINGS.

asparagus tip

The peak months for buying asparagus are April and May. When buying, look for firm, straight, uniform-size spears. The tips should be closed with crisp stalks. It's best to use asparagus within a few days of purchase.

This yummy breakfast dish is quick and can be served any day of the week. Ready-to-use crepes speed it along—find them near the berries in the produce section of your local grocery store.

Taste of Home
Test Kitchen

warm banana crepes

PREP/TOTAL TIME: 10 MIN.

1/2 cup butter, cubed
1/2 cup packed brown sugar
4 medium ripe bananas, halved lengthwise
4 prepared crepes (9 inches)

1 In a large skillet, melt butter. Add brown sugar; heat and stir until sugar is dissolved. Add bananas; cook until light golden brown, turning once.

2 In an small ungreased skillet, heat crepes for about 10 seconds on each side or until warm.

3 Place two banana halves in the center of each crepe. Fold sides over filling and roll up; drizzle with brown sugar mixture.

YIELD: 4 SERVINGS.

coconut pecan waffles

PREP/TOTAL TIME: 20 MIN.

Toasted coconut and pecans add a nutty taste to these delicious waffles. Give them a try the next time you're warming up the waffle iron.

Taste of Home Test Kitchen

2 cups biscuit/baking mix
2 eggs, lightly beaten
1/2 cup canola oil
1 cup club soda
1/4 to 1/2 teaspoon coconut extract
1/2 cup flaked coconut, toasted
1/2 cup chopped pecans, toasted

1 In a large bowl, combine the biscuit mix, eggs and oil. Add club soda and coconut extract; stir until smooth. Gently fold in the coconut and pecans.

2 Bake in a preheated waffle iron according to manufacturer's directions until golden brown.

YIELD: 12 WAFFLES.

rhubarb biscuit coffee cakes

PREP: 45 MIN. BAKE: 30 MIN.

10 tubes (12 ounces each) refrigerated
    buttermilk biscuits

20 cups sliced fresh or frozen rhubarb
    (about 6 pounds)

2-1/2 cups sugar

5 teaspoons cornstarch

10 eggs, lightly beaten

5 cartons (16 ounces each) sour cream

1 pint heavy whipping cream

2-1/2 teaspoons vanilla extract

TOPPING:

3 tablespoons sugar

1-3/4 teaspoons ground cinnamon

1 Divide biscuits among 10 ungreased 9-in. pie plates; top each with 2 cups rhubarb. In a large bowl, combine the sugar, cornstarch, eggs, sour cream, cream and vanilla. Beat on high for 2 minutes; pour over rhubarb.

2 Combine sugar and cinnamon; sprinkle over filling. Bake, uncovered, at 350° for 30-35 minutes or until golden brown and set. Remove to wire racks. Serve warm. Refrigerate leftovers.

YIELD: 10 COFFEE CAKES (8 SERVINGS EACH).

EDITOR'S NOTE: If using frozen rhubarb, measure rhubarb while still frozen, then thaw completely. Drain in a colander, but do not press liquid out.

Nothing beats the home-style taste of golden-brown fritters. This version offers diced ham and kernels of corn, and it uses a biscuit mix for fast assembly.

Nancy Foust
Stoneboro, PA

corn 'n' ham fritters

PREP/TOTAL TIME: 30 MIN.

1 cup biscuit/baking mix
1/2 teaspoon sugar
1 egg
1/2 cup whole milk
1 cup frozen corn, thawed
1/2 cup finely diced fully cooked ham
Oil for deep-fat frying
Maple syrup, optional

1 In a small bowl, combine the biscuit mix and sugar. In another bowl, whisk the egg and milk; stir into dry ingredients just until moistened. Fold in corn and ham.

2 In an electric skillet, heat 1-1/2 in. of oil to 375°. Drop batter by rounded tablespoonfuls, a few at a time, into hot oil. Fry until golden brown, about 1 minute on each side. Drain on paper towels. Serve warm with syrup if desired.

YIELD: 16 FRITTERS.

sausage egg bake

PREP: 25 MIN. BAKE: 25 MIN.

Here's a busy-day breakfast dish that's fast, flavorful and fun-to-make. The added bonus is that it uses up leftover hard-cooked eggs. Breakfast dishes always go over well at our house. This one's so easy and filling, we sometimes have it for dinner, too.

Erika Anderson • Wausau, WI

1/2 pound bulk pork sausage
3 tablespoons butter, melted, divided
2 tablespoons all-purpose flour
1/4 teaspoon salt
1/4 teaspoon pepper
1-1/4 cups whole milk
2 cups frozen shredded hash brown potatoes
4 hard-cooked eggs, sliced
1/2 cup crushed cornflakes
1/4 cup sliced green onions

1 In a large skillet, cook sausage over medium heat until no longer pink; drain. Stir in 2 tablespoons butter, flour, salt and pepper until blended.

This savory quiche is a snap to create with a convenient pastry shell crust and a can of broccoli and cheese soup. Pair it with fresh fruit at breakfast or lunch.

Barbara Cusimano
Manchester, CT

2 Gradually add milk. Bring to a boil; cook and stir for 2 minutes or until thickened. Stir in the hash browns and eggs. Transfer to a greased 1-qt. baking dish.

3 Toss cornflakes and remaining butter; sprinkle over sausage. Bake, uncovered, at 350° for 25-30 minutes or until heated. Sprinkle with onions.

YIELD: 3 SERVINGS.

a good egg

According to the American Egg Board, fresh eggs can be stored in their carton in the refrigerator for 4 to 5 weeks beyond the pack date. Some manufacturers stamp their cartons with a date 30 days beyond the pack date.

cheddar broccoli quiche

PREP: 10 MIN. BAKE: 35 MIN.

1 pastry shell (9 inches), baked
1 cup (4 ounces) shredded cheddar cheese, divided
6 eggs
1 can (10-3/4 ounces) condensed cream of broccoli and cheese soup, undiluted
2/3 cup whole milk

1 Sprinkle pastry shell with 1/2 cup cheese. In a large bowl, combine the eggs, soup and milk. Pour into crust. Cover edges loosely with foil.

2 Bake at 350° for 30 minutes. Sprinkle with remaining cheese; bake 5-10 minutes longer or until a knife inserted near the center comes out clean. Let stand for 5 minutes before cutting.

YIELD: 6-8 SERVINGS.

cherry crescent coffee cake

PREP: 25 MIN. BAKE: 15 MIN.

1 package (8 ounces) cream cheese, softened

3/4 cup confectioners' sugar, divided

1 egg

1/2 teaspoon vanilla extract

2 tubes (8 ounces each) refrigerated crescent rolls

1 can (21 ounces) cherry pie filling

2 to 3 teaspoons whole milk

1 In a small bowl, beat cream cheese and 1/4 cup confectioners' sugar until smooth. Add egg; beat just until combined. Stir in vanilla; set aside.

2 Unroll crescent dough and separate into triangles. Set four triangles aside. Place remaining triangles on a greased 14-in. pizza pan, forming a ring with wide ends facing outer edge of pan and pointed ends toward the center; leave a 3-in. hole in the center. Lightly press seams together.

3 Spread cream cheese mixture over dough to within 1/2 in. of edges. Top with pie filling to within 1/2 in. of cream cheese edges. Cut reserved triangles into thirds, starting at the wide end and ending at the point. Arrange over pie filling with points facing outer edge of pan, forming spokes. Press ends at center and outer edge to seal.

4 Bake at 375° for 15-20 minutes or until golden brown. Cool on a wire rack. Combine remaining confectioners' sugar and enough milk to achieve drizzling consistency; drizzle over warm coffee cake.

YIELD: 12 SERVINGS.

chili-cheese breakfast bake

PREP: 20 MIN. + CHILLING BAKE: 1 HOUR

Get everyone out of bed on nippy fall mornings with this savory Southwest-flavored breakfast casserole.

Kathy Mead • Surprise, AZ

6 slices whole wheat bread, cubed

1/2 cup shredded reduced-fat Mexican cheese blend

1 can (4 ounces) chopped green chilies

4 eggs

4 egg whites

2 cups fat-free milk

1 teaspoon ground mustard

1/2 teaspoon salt

Dash pepper

1 In a 1-1/2-qt. baking dish coated with cooking spray, layer half of the bread cubes, cheese and chilies. Repeat layers. In a large bowl, whisk the eggs, egg whites, milk, mustard, salt and pepper; pour over top. Cover and refrigerate overnight.

2 Remove from the refrigerator 30 minutes before baking. Bake, uncovered, at 350° for 60-70 minutes or until a knife inserted near the center comes out clean. Let stand for 5 minutes before cutting.

YIELD: 4 SERVINGS.

My husband needs to watch what he eats, so I like to find wholesome recipes that are easy to prepare. I enjoy treating him with these tender rolls.
Lacey Griffin • Fredonia, PA

orange marmalade sweet rolls

PREP: 15 MIN. + RISING BAKE: 15 MIN.

1 loaf (1 pound) frozen bread dough, thawed

1/3 cup 100% orange marmalade spreadable fruit

2 tablespoons raisins

1/3 cup confectioners' sugar

1/2 teaspoon grated orange peel

2 teaspoons orange juice

1 On a floured surface, roll dough into a 12-in. x 8-in. rectangle; brush with spreadable fruit. Sprinkle with raisins. Roll up jelly-roll style, starting with a long side; pinch seam to seal.

2 Cut into 12 slices. Place cut side down in muffin cups coated with cooking spray. Cover and let rise until doubled, about 45 minutes.

3 Bake at 350° for 15-20 minutes or until golden brown. Immediately invert onto serving plates. Combine the confectioners' sugar, orange peel and orange juice; drizzle over warm rolls.

YIELD: 12 SERVINGS.

Bursting with poppy seeds, these luscious muffins are filled and drizzled with lots of lemony flavor. They're great with coffee or tea and couldn't be much easier to whip up.

Donna Gonda
North Canton, OH

sweet sunshine breakfast muffins

PREP/TOTAL TIME: 30 MIN.

2 cups biscuit/baking mix

1 package (3.4 ounces) instant lemon pudding mix

1/4 cup poppy seeds

1/4 teaspoon grated lemon peel

2 eggs

1 cup milk

1/4 cup canola oil

3/4 cup confectioners' sugar

1 tablespoon lemon juice

1 In a large bowl, combine the baking mix, pudding mix, poppy seeds and lemon peel. In another bowl, combine the eggs, milk and oil; stir into dry ingredients just until moistened. Fill greased or paper-lined muffin cups two-thirds full.

2 Bake at 375° for 20-25 minutes or until a toothpick inserted near the center comes out clean. Cool for 5 minutes before removing from pan to a wire rack.

3 In a small bowl, combine confectioners' sugar and lemon juice; drizzle over muffins.

YIELD: 1 DOZEN.

easy potato pancakes

PREP/TOTAL TIME: 20 MIN.

3 cups frozen shredded hash brown potatoes

2 tablespoons all-purpose flour

2 eggs, lightly beaten

3 tablespoons butter, melted

1-1/2 teaspoons water

1/2 teaspoon salt

1 tablespoon canola oil

1 Place the hash browns in a strainer; rinse with cold water until thawed. Drain thoroughly; transfer to a large bowl. Add the flour, eggs, butter, water and salt; mix well.

2 Heat oil in a large skillet over medium heat. Drop batter by 1/3 cupfuls into oil; fry until golden brown on both sides. Drain on paper towels.

YIELD: 4 SERVINGS.

melted butter

When melted butter is called for, the butter is measured first and then melted. The convenient markings on the wrappers make it easy to slice off the amount you need and melt it.

These supper-time sidekicks pack a lot of pizzazz. This chapter is full of vegetable casseroles, rice dishes and more to help you round out your menu.

standout side dishes

spicy beans and rice

PREP/TOTAL TIME: 25 MIN.

2 cups uncooked instant rice

2 cups water

1/2 teaspoon garlic powder

1/2 teaspoon chili powder

1/2 teaspoon ground cumin

Dash pepper

1 can (16 ounces) chili beans, undrained

1 can (11 ounces) Mexicorn, drained

1 can (10 ounces) diced tomatoes and green chilies, drained

1/2 cup salsa

1 cup (4 ounces) shredded reduced-fat cheddar cheese

1 In a 2-qt. microwave-safe dish, combine the first six ingredients; cover and microwave on high for 5-7 minutes or until water is absorbed.

2 Stir in the beans, Mexicorn, tomatoes and salsa; top with cheese. Cover and microwave on high 2-3 minutes longer or until heated through and cheese is melted.

YIELD: 6 SERVINGS.

For an eye-appealing twist on traditional mashed potatoes, serve this tempting side with ham, chicken or your favorite meat loaf.

Taste of Home Test Kitchen

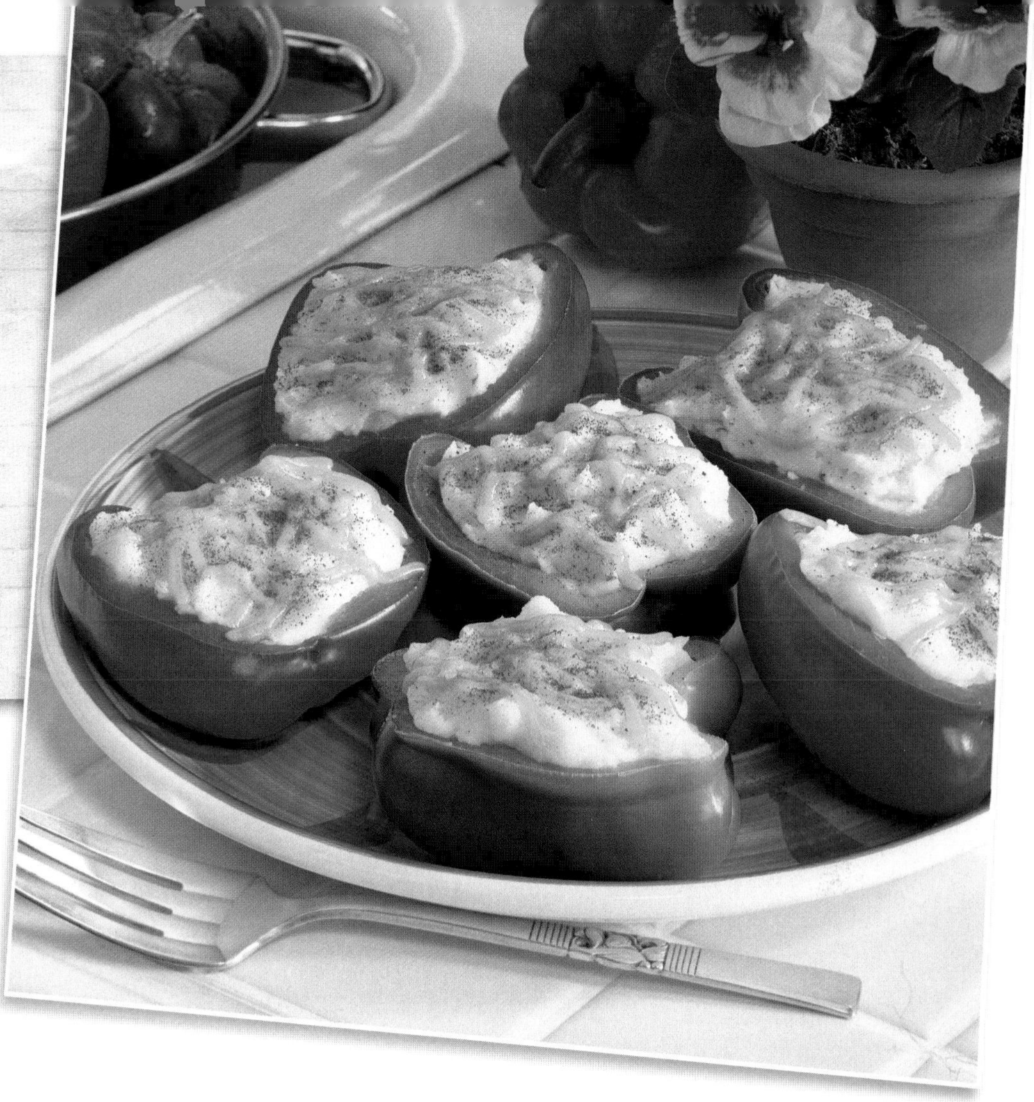

potato-stuffed peppers

PREP/ TOTAL TIME: 30 MIN.

1 package (22 ounces) frozen mashed potatoes
2 cups whole milk
2 tablespoons butter
1 envelope ranch salad dressing mix
Pepper to taste
4 medium green or red sweet peppers
1 cup (4 ounces) shredded cheddar cheese
Paprika

1 Prepare potatoes with milk and butter according to package directions. Stir in dressing mix and season with pepper; set aside.

2 Cut peppers in half lengthwise; do not remove the tops. Remove stems and seeds. Place in an ungreased microwave-safe 13-in. x 9-in. dish.

3 Cover and microwave on high for 5 minutes. Spoon potatoes into pepper halves. Cover and microwave on high for 3-4 minutes or until peppers are tender. Sprinkle with cheese and paprika.

YIELD: 8 SERVINGS.

potatoes, peas & pearl onions

PREP/TOTAL TIME: 20 MIN.

1 package (20 ounces) refrigerated red potato wedges

1/3 cup water

1-1/3 cups frozen pearl onions, thawed

3 tablespoons butter

2/3 cup heavy whipping cream

1/3 cup chicken broth

1/4 teaspoon salt

1/4 teaspoon ground nutmeg

1/4 teaspoon pepper

2/3 cup frozen peas, thawed

3 tablespoons chopped green onions

1 Place potatoes and water in a 2-qt. microwave-safe bowl. Cover and microwave on high for 8-10 minutes or until potatoes are tender; drain and set aside.

2 Meanwhile, in a large skillet, saute pearl onions in butter for 2 minutes. Add the cream, broth, salt, nutmeg and pepper. Bring to a boil. Reduce heat; simmer, uncovered, for 5-7 minutes or until onions are tender. Stir in the peas, green onions and reserved potatoes; heat through.

YIELD: 6 SERVINGS.

EDITOR'S NOTE: This recipe was tested in a 1,100-watt microwave.

deluxe scalloped corn

PREP: 10 MIN. BAKE: 30 MIN.

I dress up canned corn with cream of mushroom soup and sour cream for this speedy baked side. With a savory cracker coating, the recipe yields many servings and is made in a big pan, so it's perfect for a potluck or larger gathering.

Shawna Hull • Grovetown, GA

4 cans (15-1/4 ounces each) whole kernel corn, drained

1 can (10-3/4 ounces) condensed cream of mushroom soup, undiluted

1 cup (8 ounces) sour cream

1/4 cup all-purpose flour

1/4 cup whole milk

1 tablespoon dried minced onion

1/4 teaspoon salt

1/4 teaspoon pepper

1-3/4 cups crushed butter-flavored crackers (about 34 crackers)

1 cup (4 ounces) shredded cheddar cheese

1 In a large bowl, combine the first eight ingredients. Transfer to a greased 13-in. x 9-in. baking dish. Combine cracker crumbs and cheese; sprinkle over the top.

2 Bake, uncovered, at 350° for 30-35 minutes or until edges are bubbly.

YIELD: 8-10 SERVINGS.

My teenage sons love this creamy side dish so much, they'll eat it regardless of which vegetables I use.

Karen Hoyle • Excelsior, MN

kudos to orzo

Because of orzo's similar shape and mild flavor, it can be used for rice in many recipes. Ounce for ounce, rice and orzo contain similar amounts of fat, sugar, carbohydrates and even sodium.

caesar orzo with asparagus

PREP/TOTAL TIME: 25 MIN.

2 cans (14-1/2 ounces each) reduced-sodium chicken broth

2 cups water

2 cups uncooked orzo pasta

2 pounds fresh asparagus, trimmed and cut into 2-inch pieces

2/3 cup fat-free creamy Caesar salad dressing

2/3 cup shredded Parmesan cheese

1 In a large saucepan, bring broth and water to a boil. Add orzo; cook and stir for 3 minutes. Add asparagus. Cook, uncovered, over medium heat for 6-8 minutes or until orzo and asparagus are tender, stirring frequently; drain. Stir in salad dressing and cheese; toss to coat.

YIELD: 12 SERVINGS.

apricot almond dressing

PREP: 20 MIN. BAKE: 35 MIN.

2 cups chopped onions

2 cups chopped celery

1/2 cup slivered almonds

1/2 cup butter

1 can (14-1/2 ounces) chicken broth

1 package (12 ounces) unseasoned stuffing cubes

1/4 cup chopped dried apricots

1 teaspoon each rubbed sage, dried thyme and dried rosemary, crushed

Salt and pepper to taste

1 In a large skillet, saute the onions, celery and almonds in butter until the vegetables are tender. Stir in the broth, stuffing, apricots and seasonings.

2 Spoon into a greased 3-qt. baking dish. Cover and bake at 350° for 30 minutes. Uncover and bake 5-10 minutes longer or until heated through.

YIELD: 10 SERVINGS.

flavorful oniony asparagus

PREP/TOTAL TIME: 20 MIN.

2 pounds fresh asparagus, trimmed
1/4 cup butter, cubed
1 tablespoon onion soup mix
1/2 cup shredded part-skim mozzarella cheese

1 Place asparagus in a steamer basket. Place in a large saucepan or skillet over 1 in. of water; bring to a boil. Cover and steam for 4-5 minutes or until crisp-tender.

2 In a small saucepan, melt butter. Add soup mix. Cook and stir for 1 minute or until heated through. Remove asparagus to a serving dish. Drizzle with butter mixture; sprinkle with cheese.

YIELD: 8-10 SERVINGS.

As a working mom with four children, I don't have much time to cook big meals during the week. But on Sundays, when I make a special meal, this is our favorite way to enjoy asparagus.

Kathy Mitchell • Tinley Park, IL

microwave corn 'n' bean bake

PREP/TOTAL TIME: 20 MIN.

This is such an easy dish to make, it will become a weekly tradition. Best of all, it fits every menu, no matter what the season.

Nellie Perdue • Summer Shade, KY

1 package (16 ounces) frozen cut green beans
1 can (15-1/4 ounces) whole kernel corn, drained
1 can (10-3/4 ounces) condensed cream of mushroom soup, undiluted
1 cup (4 ounces) shredded cheddar cheese, divided
1/2 cup crushed butter-flavored crackers (about 12 crackers)

1 In a bowl, combine the beans, corn, soup and 1/2 cup cheese. Spoon into a greased 2-qt. microwave-safe dish. Cover and microwave on high for 10 minutes, stirring once. Combine cracker crumbs and remaining cheese; sprinkle over beans. Microwave, uncovered, on high for 3-5 minutes or until beans are tender.

YIELD: 6 SERVINGS.

EDITOR'S NOTE: This recipe was tested in a 1,100-watt microwave.

microwaving

A higher-wattage microwave cooks faster than a lower-wattage one, so adjust the time that's needed to prepare dishes in your microwave. As a general guide, start with a time about two-thirds of what's called for.

pierogi pasta shells

PREP: 30 MIN. BAKE: 30 MIN.

51 uncooked jumbo pasta shells

3 packages (24 ounces each) refrigerated mashed potatoes

2 tablespoons dried minced onion

1/2 teaspoon onion powder

1/2 teaspoon garlic powder

4 cups (16 ounces) shredded cheddar cheese, divided

1/2 cup chopped green onions

1 Cook pasta shells according to package directions; drain and rinse in cold water. Place mashed potatoes in a large microwave-safe bowl. Cover and microwave on high for 4 minutes, stirring once. Add the minced onion, onion powder and garlic powder. Stir in 2 cups of cheese until blended.

2 Stuff into shells. Place in two greased 13-in. x 9-in. baking dishes. Sprinkle with green onions and remaining cheese. Cover and bake at 350° for 20 minutes. Uncover; bake 10 minutes longer or until heated through.

YIELD: 17 SERVINGS.

I came up with this family favorite when I needed to use up leftover baked potatoes and extra produce from our garden. It's a great-tasting side dish. My husband requests it all the time and brags about it to company.

Jenelle Parks
Hayfield, MN

herbed potatoes and veggies

PREP/TOTAL TIME: 25 MIN.

4 medium baking potatoes
1-1/2 cups diced zucchini
3 tablespoons olive oil
2 tablespoons plus 1 teaspoon savory herb with garlic soup mix
1/4 teaspoon pepper
10 cherry tomatoes, halved

1 Scrub and pierce potatoes; place on a microwave-safe plate. Cover and microwave on high for 5-6 minutes on each side or until tender. When potatoes are cool enough to handle, cut into cubes.

2 In a large skillet, saute potatoes and zucchini in oil for 5 minutes or until vegetables are tender. Sprinkle with soup mix and pepper. Cook until heated through, stirring occasionally. Add tomatoes; cook 1 minute longer.

YIELD: 6 SERVINGS.

EDITOR'S NOTE: This recipe was tested in a 1,100-watt microwave.

herbed steak fries

PREP/TOTAL TIME: 25 MIN.

4 cups frozen steak fries
1 tablespoon olive oil
1-1/2 teaspoons dried basil
1-1/2 teaspoons dried parsley flakes
1/4 teaspoon garlic salt
1/4 teaspoon seasoned salt
1/4 cup grated Romano cheese

1 In a large bowl, combine the first six ingredients; toss to coat. Arrange steak fries in a single layer in a greased 15-in. x 10-in. x 1-in. baking pan.

2 Bake at 450° for 15-20 minutes or until lightly browned. Sprinkle with cheese.

YIELD: 4 SERVINGS.

saucy baked beans

PREP: 10 MIN. BAKE: 1-1/4 HOURS

My family enjoys these baked beans with corn bread, but they also round out any cookout. Canned pork and beans make preparation easy.

Phyllis Schmalz • Kansas City, KS

2 cans (31 ounces each) pork and beans
1-1/2 cups packed brown sugar
1/2 pound sliced bacon, cooked and crumbled
1 cup finely chopped onion
1 cup ketchup
1 cup cola
2 tablespoons ground mustard

1 In a large bowl, combine all ingredients. Pour into a greased 3-qt. baking dish. Bake, uncovered, at 325° for 1-1/4 hours or until bubbly.

YIELD: 12-15 SERVINGS.

creamy tortellini

PREP/TOTAL TIME: 25 MIN.

3 cups refrigerated cheese tortellini
2 teaspoons minced garlic
2 tablespoons canola oil
1 envelope vegetable soup mix
2 cups half-and-half cream
1/4 cup minced fresh parsley
1/4 cup shredded part-skim mozzarella cheese
1/4 teaspoon pepper

1 Cook tortellini according to package directions. Meanwhile, in a large skillet, saute garlic in oil until tender. Combine soup mix and cream; stir into skillet.

2 Drain tortellini; add to cream mixture. Bring to a boil. Reduce heat; simmer, uncovered, for 4-5 minutes or until heated through, stirring occasionally.

3 Add the parsley, cheese and pepper. Cook 3-4 minutes longer or until cheese is melted.

YIELD: 6-8 SERVINGS.

chili-cheese mashed potatoes

PREP/TOTAL TIME: 10 MIN.

This appetizing spin on traditional mashed potatoes will shine on the dinner table.

Peter Halferty • Corpus Christi, TX

2-3/4 cups water
1 cup fat-free milk
1-1/2 teaspoons salt
1 tablespoon butter
3 garlic cloves, minced
3 cups instant mashed potato flakes
2 cans (4 ounces each) chopped green chilies
1 cup (4 ounces) shredded reduced-fat Mexican cheese blend

1 In a large saucepan, bring the water, milk and salt to a boil. Add the butter, garlic, potato flakes and chilies; stir until thickened. Sprinkle with cheese.

YIELD: 6 SERVINGS.

I adapted this dish from my mom's recipe. You can also add cooked shrimp or seafood for a satisfying one-dish meal. It's delicious.
Bob Gebhardt • Wausau, WI

corn bread pudding

PREP: 5 MIN. BAKE: 40 MIN.

2 eggs
1 cup (8 ounces) sour cream
1 can (15-1/4 ounces) whole kernel corn, drained
1 can (14-3/4 ounces) cream-style corn
1/2 cup butter, melted
1 package (8-1/2 ounces) corn bread/muffin mix
1/4 teaspoon paprika

1 In a large bowl, combine the first five ingredients. Stir in corn bread mix just until blended. Pour into a greased 3-qt. baking dish. Sprinkle with paprika.

2 Bake, uncovered, at 350° for 40-45 minutes or until a knife inserted near the center. Serve warm.

YIELD: 12 SERVINGS.

minced garlic
To mince fresh garlic, crush the garlic cloves with the blade of your chef's knife. You may need to crush each garlic clove separately. Peel away the skin, then chop or mince as directed.

For a worthy side dish, offer up this tasty combination of pasta and vegetables coated in a flavorful Szechuan sauce. The ginger comes through nicely. If you like spicy food, add 1/4 teaspoon crushed red pepper with the ginger.

Debbie Stadtler
Fredericksburg, VA

skillet lo mein

PREP/TOTAL TIME: 20 MIN.

4 ounces uncooked spaghetti, broken into thirds

1 tablespoon canola oil

1 package (9 ounces) frozen Szechuan stir-fry vegetables with sauce, thawed

1/3 cup julienned carrot

1/4 cup sliced celery

1/4 cup sliced onion

2 tablespoons reduced-sodium soy sauce

1/8 teaspoon ground ginger

1 Cook spaghetti according to package directions. Meanwhile, in a large skillet, heat oil over medium-high heat; stir in the stir-fry vegetables, contents of seasoning packet, carrot, celery, onion, soy sauce and ginger. Bring to a boil.

2 Reduce heat; simmer, uncovered, for 3-4 minutes or until vegetables are crisp-tender. Drain spaghetti; stir into vegetable mixture.

YIELD: 4 SERVINGS.

A dear friend shared this recipe with me years ago. My family enjoys it with meat entrees as a substitute for potatoes. It's great to take to a potluck for a dish to pass, but be prepared to also pass along the recipe!

Melba Cleveland
Groveland, CA

mushroom barley casserole

PREP: 10 MIN. BAKE: 1-1/4 HOURS

1 cup medium pearl barley

1 small onion, chopped

1/4 cup butter

1-1/2 cups sliced fresh mushrooms

1 cup slivered almonds, toasted

1 envelope onion soup mix

2 tablespoons minced fresh parsley or
   2 teaspoons dried parsley flakes

3 to 3-1/2 cups chicken broth

1 In a small skillet, saute barley and onion in butter for 5 minutes or until onion is tender. Transfer to an ungreased 2-qt. baking dish. Stir in the mushrooms, almonds, soup mix and parsley. Add 3 cups broth.

2 Bake, uncovered, at 350° for 1-1/4 hours or until barley is tender, adding more broth if needed.

YIELD: 8-10 SERVINGS.

These fresh-tasting stuffed tomatoes make a lovely side dish or hearty appetizer. You'll appreciate the simplicity and quickness of this recipe.

Taste of Home Test Kitchen

broiled tomatoes with artichokes

PREP/TOTAL TIME: 15 MIN.

3 small tomatoes, halved

1 jar (7-1/2 ounces) marinated artichoke hearts, drained and chopped

1/2 cup crumbled feta cheese

1/3 cup dry bread crumbs

2 tablespoons butter, melted

1 Cut a thin slice off the top of each tomato. Scoop out pulp, leaving a 1/2-in. shell. Invert onto paper towels to drain.

2 Place cut side up on a foil-lined baking sheet. Combine the artichokes and cheese; place 2 tablespoons in the center of each tomato. Broil 3-4 in. from the heat for 2-3 minutes or until bubbly.

3 Toss the bread crumbs and butter; sprinkle over tomatoes. Broil 3-4 in. from the heat for 1-2 minutes or until browned.

YIELD: 6 SERVINGS.

broccoli casserole

PREP: 20 MIN. BAKE: 35 MIN.

- 2 packages (16 ounces each) frozen broccoli florets
- 1 can (10-3/4 ounces) condensed cream of mushroom soup, undiluted
- 1 cup (8 ounces) sour cream
- 1-1/2 cups (6 ounces) shredded sharp cheddar cheese, divided
- 1 can (6 ounces) french-fried onions, divided

1 Cook broccoli according to package directions; drain well. In a large saucepan, combine the soup, sour cream, 1 cup cheese and 1-1/4 cups onions. Cook over medium heat for 4-5 minutes or until heated through. Stir in the broccoli.

2 Pour into a greased 2-qt. baking dish. Bake, uncovered, at 325° for 25-30 minutes or until bubbly. Sprinkle with the remaining cheese and onions. Bake 10-15 minutes longer or until cheese is melted.

YIELD: 6-8 SERVINGS.

hot dish to go

An easy way to transport a casserole is to put the dish inside a clear plastic oven bag. The bags trap any spills, don't melt and people can see what's inside. It's so easy to slide the dish in and seal it with a twist tie.

Make most any meal better with Loaded Waffle Fries. I top them with a savory blend of cheese, scallions and bacon. I copied this family favorite from a local restaurant, and I found that it's great with hot dogs, burgers or even by itself.

Jeffrey Viccone
Decatur, IL

loaded waffle fries

PREP/TOTAL TIME: 30 MIN.

4 cups frozen waffle-cut fries
1/2 to 1-1/2 teaspoons steak seasoning
1 cup (4 ounces) shredded cheddar cheese
2 tablespoons chopped green onions
2 tablespoons real bacon bits

1 Arrange waffle fries in a greased 15-in. x 10-in. x 1-in. baking pan. Bake at 450° for 20-25 minutes or until lightly browned.

2 Sprinkle with steak seasoning; toss to coat. Top with cheese, onions and bacon. Bake 2-3 minutes longer or until cheese is melted.

YIELD: 4 SERVINGS.

EDITOR'S NOTE: This recipe was tested with McCormick's Montreal Steak Seasoning. Look for it in the spice aisle.

shredded potato casserole

PREP: 10 MIN. BAKE: 45 MIN.

1 can (10-3/4 ounces) condensed cream of mushroom soup, undiluted

1 cup (8 ounces) sour cream

1/2 cup whole milk

1 cup (4 ounces) shredded cheddar cheese

1/2 cup butter, melted, divided

1 package (30 ounces) frozen shredded hash brown potatoes, thawed

1 cup cornflake crumbs

1/4 cup grated Parmesan cheese

1 In a large bowl, combine the soup, sour cream, milk, cheddar cheese and 1/4 cup butter. Stir in the hash browns. Transfer to a greased 13-in. x 9-in. baking dish.

2 In a small bowl, combine the cornflake crumbs, Parmesan cheese and remaining butter; sprinkle over top. Bake, uncovered, at 325° for 45-50 minutes or until heated through.

YIELD: 6-8 SERVINGS.

mini green bean casserole

PREP/TOTAL TIME: 20 MIN.

Everyone loves green bean casserole for the holidays and this quick-to-fix version is perfect for everyday dinners.

Christy Hinrichs • Parkville, MS

1/2 cup condensed cream of mushroom soup, undiluted

3 tablespoons 2% milk

1/2 teaspoon reduced-sodium soy sauce

Dash pepper

1-1/3 cups frozen cut green beans, thawed

1/2 cup french-fried onions, divided

1 In a small bowl, combine the soup, milk, soy sauce and pepper. Stir in green beans and 1/4 cup onions.

2 Transfer to a 2-cup baking dish coated with cooking spray. Sprinkle with remaining onions. Bake, uncovered, at 400° for 12-15 minutes or until bubbly.

YIELD: 2 SERVINGS.

This recipe works best with thinly sliced cabbage, so it is best not to use a shredder.
Taste of Home Test Kitchen

cabbage capers

When buying cabbage, look for heavy heads with crisp-looking, firmly packed leaves. Refrigerate tightly wrapped in a plastic bag for up to 2 weeks. A 1-1/2-pound cabbage will yield 8 cups sliced or shredded.

pineapple cabbage saute

PREP/TOTAL TIME: 20 MIN.

1 can (8 ounces) crushed pineapple

6 cups thinly sliced cabbage

1 tablespoon olive oil

2 tablespoons honey mustard salad dressing

1/8 teaspoon white pepper

1 Drain pineapple, reserving 1 tablespoon juice; set aside. In a large skillet, saute cabbage in oil for 5-8 minutes or until crisp-tender. Add the salad dressing, pepper and reserved pineapple and juice. Cook for 1 minute or until heated through.

YIELD: 6 SERVINGS

You can serve this homey blend of fresh green beans, potato wedges and chopped red onion hot or cold. Either way, this easy side dish makes a pleasing accompaniment to Mom's meat loaf or almost any other meat.

Daria Burcar
Rochester, MI

red potatoes with beans

PREP/TOTAL TIME: 20 MIN.

1-1/3 pounds fresh green beans, trimmed
1/3 cup water
6 small red potatoes, cut into wedges
1/2 cup chopped red onion
1/2 cup Italian salad dressing

1 Place the beans and water in a 2-qt. microwave-safe dish. Cover and microwave on high for 6-8 minutes or until tender.

2 Meanwhile, place the potatoes in a large saucepan and cover with water. Bring to a boil. Reduce heat; cover and cook for 5-7 minutes or until tender. Drain beans and potatoes; place in a bowl. Add onion and dressing; toss to coat.

YIELD: 8 SERVINGS.

wild rice pepper salad

PREP: 10 MIN. COOK: 1 HOUR + CHILLING

2/3 cup uncooked wild rice

3 cups water

1 cup chopped green pepper

1 cup chopped sweet red pepper

1 cup chopped sweet yellow pepper

1/2 cup sunflower kernels

1/3 cup chopped onion

1/3 cup raisins

1/2 cup fat-free Italian salad dressing

1 In a small saucepan, bring the rice and water to a boil. Reduce heat; cover and simmer for 1 hour or until rice is tender. Drain and place in a bowl. Refrigerate until chilled. Add the remaining ingredients; toss to coat.

YIELD: 6 SERVINGS.

saucy potatoes with ham

PREP: 10 MIN. BAKE: 65 MIN.

1 can (10-3/4 ounces) condensed cream of potato soup, undiluted

1/2 cup heavy whipping cream

1/2 teaspoon salt

1/4 teaspoon pepper

4 large red potatoes, thinly sliced

1 cup cubed fully cooked ham

1/2 cup thinly sliced green onions with tops

1/2 cup salad croutons, crushed

1 In a large bowl, combine the soup, cream, salt and pepper. Fold in the potatoes, ham and onions. Transfer to a greased 2-qt. baking dish.

2 Cover and bake at 350° for 50 minutes. Uncover; sprinkle with croutons. Bake 15-20 minutes longer or until potatoes are tender and topping is golden brown.

YIELD: 6-8 SERVINGS.

creamed spinach

PREP/TOTAL TIME: 20 MIN.

This flavorful accompaniment is so tasty, you'll forget that it features nutritious spinach. It's a family favorite for holidays and special occasions. It pairs well with roasted turkey, chicken, ham or brisket.

Elizabeth Hunter • Flower Mounds, TX

- 2 packages (10 ounces each) frozen chopped spinach
- 1 tablespoon dried minced onion
- 1 tablespoon all-purpose flour
- 1 can condensed cream of celery soup, undiluted
- 1/4 cup butter, cubed
- 1/4 teaspoon garlic powder
- Dash pepper

1 Cook spinach according to package directions; drain and squeeze dry. Add onion; set aside. In a large saucepan, combine the flour, soup, butter and garlic powder. Bring to a boil over medium heat; cook and stir for 1 minute or until thickened. Stir in spinach mixture and pepper.

YIELD: 3-4 SERVINGS.

This few-ingredient dish is a sure favorite, no matter what the main course may be. Spicy Mexican cheese dip from the snack aisle creates a zippy coating for the fun pasta.

JoAnne Palmer • Mechanicsville, MD

pasta pointer
To cook pasta more evenly, prevent it from sticking together and avoid boil-overs, always cook pasta in a large kettle or Dutch oven. Unless you have a very large kettle, don't cook more than 2 pounds of pasta at a time.

con queso spirals

PREP/TOTAL TIME: 20 MIN.

- 2-1/2 cups uncooked spiral pasta
- 1 tablespoon butter
- 1 cup salsa con queso dip
- Sour cream

1 Cook pasta according to package directions; drain. Place in a bowl; stir in butter until melted. Stir in con queso dip. Serve with sour cream.

YIELD: 4 SERVINGS.

buttery almond green beans

PREP/TOTAL TIME: 30 MIN.

2 pounds fresh green beans, trimmed

2 cups water

1 envelope onion soup mix

2/3 cup slivered almonds, toasted

2 tablespoons grated Parmesan cheese

1 teaspoon paprika

6 tablespoons butter, melted

1 In a large saucepan, combine the beans, water and soup mix. Bring to a boil. Reduce heat; cover and simmer for 15-20 minutes or until beans are crisp-tender.

2 In a small bowl, combine the almonds, cheese and paprika. Drain beans; drizzle with butter and sprinkle with almond mixture. Toss to coat.

YIELD: 8 SERVINGS.

For quicker preparation, purchase ready-to-use cauliflowerets. Packages can be found in the produce section of your local grocery store.

Taste of Home
Test Kitchen

cauliflower au gratin

PREP/TOTAL TIME: 25 MIN.

1 cup chicken broth
1 large head cauliflower, broken into florets
1/4 cup butter, cubed
1/4 cup seasoned bread crumbs
1/2 cup shredded Parmesan cheese

1 In a large saucepan, bring broth to a boil. Add cauliflower. Reduce heat to medium; cover and cook for 15-18 minutes or until tender.

2 Meanwhile, in a small skillet, melt butter. Add bread crumbs; cook and stir for 3-5 minutes or until toasted and browned. Remove from the heat; stir in Parmesan cheese. Drain cauliflower; top with crumb mixture.

YIELD: 6 SERVINGS.

It's a cinch to make bread all year-round with the irresistible, straightforward recipes in this chapter. They'll add the perfect touch to your meal!

bountiful breads

This recipe is too good not to share! Three loaves easily feed a crowd, or you can use them as gifts. Either way, these spice-swirled loaves get gobbled up fast.

Robin Guthrie
Victorville, CA

pumpkin pecan loaves

PREP: 20 MIN. BAKE: 45 MIN. + COOLING

3/4 cup packed brown sugar

1/2 cup all-purpose flour

1/3 cup cold butter, cubed

1 cup chopped pecans, divided

2 packages (16 ounces each) pound cake mix

1 can (15 ounces) solid-pack pumpkin

4 eggs

3/4 cup water

2 teaspoons baking soda

2 teaspoons pumpkin pie spice

1 For streusel, combine brown sugar and flour in a bowl; cut in butter until mixture resembles coarse crumbs. Stir in 1/2 cup pecans; set aside.

2 In a large bowl, combine the pound cake mixes, pumpkin, eggs, water, baking soda and pumpkin pie spice; beat on low speed for 30 seconds. Beat on medium for 2 minutes. Fold in remaining pecans.

3 Divide half of the batter among three greased and floured 8-in. x 4-in. loaf pans. Sprinkle with half of the streusel. Top with remaining batter and streusel.

4 Bake at 350° for 45-50 minutes or until a toothpick inserted near the center comes out clean. Cool for 10 minutes before removing from pans to wire racks to cool completely.

YIELD: 3 LOAVES (12 SLICES EACH).

Everyone raves about the tasty fruit topping on these convenient refrigerated biscuits. I usually double this recipe and put it in two pie plates to serve a crowd. It really isn't hard to make the topping, but in a pinch, you can substitute canned apple pie filling instead.

Sharon Rose Ristich
Rochester, NY

apple-topped biscuits

PREP: 15 MIN. + STANDING BAKE: 20 MIN.

3 cups sliced peeled tart apples

1/3 cup sugar

1 tablespoon quick-cooking tapioca

1-1/2 teaspoons lemon juice

1/2 teaspoon ground cinnamon

1/8 teaspoon salt

1/8 teaspoon ground nutmeg

1 tube (16.3 ounces) large refrigerated
   buttermilk biscuits

1 In a large saucepan, combine the apples, sugar, tapioca, lemon juice, cinnamon, salt and nutmeg. Let stand for 15 minutes. Cook over medium heat for 8-10 minutes or until apples are tender.

2 Transfer apple mixture to a greased 9-in. pie plate. Place biscuits over apples. Bake at 375° for 18-20 minutes or until biscuits are browned. Immediately invert onto a serving plate.

YIELD: 8 SERVINGS.

zucchini
cheddar biscuits

PREP/TOTAL TIME: 25 MIN.

1 large onion, chopped
1/4 cup butter, cubed
2-1/2 cups biscuit/baking mix
1 tablespoon minced fresh parsley
1/2 teaspoon dried basil
1/2 teaspoon dried thyme
3 eggs, lightly beaten
1/4 cup whole milk
1-1/2 cups shredded zucchini
1 cup (4 ounces) shredded cheddar cheese

1 In a large skillet, saute onion in butter until tender. In a large bowl, combine the biscuit mix, parsley, basil, thyme and onion mixture. In another bowl. combine eggs and milk. Stir into biscuit mixture just until combined. Fold in zucchini and cheese.

2 Drop by 1/4 cupfuls 2 in. apart onto greased baking sheets. Bake at 400° for 10-14 minutes or until golden brown. Serve warm. Refrigerate leftovers.

YIELD: 16 BISCUITS.

breadsticks for two

PREP: 15 MIN. + RISING BAKE: 15 MIN.

This is the perfect recipe for date night. The portions are ideal for a dinner with your special someone.

Taste of Home Test Kitchen

1/3 cup grated Parmesan cheese

1/2 teaspoon dried basil

1/4 teaspoon garlic powder

1 egg white

1 teaspoon water

4 frozen bread dough dinner rolls, thawed

1 In a shallow dish, combine the cheese, basil and garlic powder. In a small bowl, whisk egg white and water. Roll each dough ball into an 8-in. rope. Dip in egg mixture, then roll in cheese mixture. Twist each rope three or four times.

2 Place on a greased baking sheet. Cover; let rise in a warm place until doubled, about 20 minutes. Bake at 350° for 12-16 minutes or until golden brown.

YIELD: 4 BREADSTICKS.

cheesy pesto bread

PREP/TOTAL TIME: 20 MIN.

1 prebaked 12-inch pizza crust

3 tablespoons prepared pesto

1/8 teaspoon garlic salt

1 cup (4 ounces) shredded mozzarella cheese

1/2 cup shredded Parmesan cheese

1 Place crust on a pizza pan or baking sheet. Spread with pesto; sprinkle with garlic salt and cheeses. Bake at 325° for 12-15 minutes or until cheese is melted. Cut into wedges.

YIELD: 6-8 SERVINGS.

chocolate-filled crescents

PREP: 25 MIN. BAKE: 15 MIN.

3 tablespoons butter, softened

1 cup confectioners' sugar

1 tablespoon whole milk

1 teaspoon vanilla extract

1/4 cup baking cocoa

3 tablespoons finely chopped pecans

2 tubes (8 ounces each) refrigerated crescent rolls

CHOCOLATE GLAZE:

1 cup confectioners' sugar

2 tablespoons baking cocoa

2 tablespoons plus 1 teaspoon water

2 tablespoons butter, melted

1/2 teaspoon vanilla extract

1 In a small bowl, cream butter and confectioners' sugar until light and fluffy. Beat in milk and vanilla. Gradually add cocoa and mix well. Stir in pecans.

2 Unroll crescent dough and separate into triangles. Spread about 2 rounded teaspoons of filling over each triangle to within 1/4 in. of edges. Roll up each from the wide end. Place point side down 2 in. apart on ungreased baking sheets. Curve ends to form crescent shapes.

3 Bake at 375° for 12-15 minutes or until golden brown. Remove to wire racks; cool slightly. In a small bowl, whisk glaze ingredients until smooth; drizzle over crescents.

YIELD: 16 SERVINGS.

apple nutmeg rolls

PREP: 20 MIN. + RISING   BAKE: 25 MIN.

Cinnamon and nutmeg add nice spice to these pinwheel rolls that are chock-full of apple chunks. Frozen bread dough lends to its fast preparation.

Richard Bunt • Painted Post, NY

1 loaf (1 pound) frozen bread dough, thawed
2 tablespoons butter, softened
1/4 cup packed brown sugar
1/4 cup finely chopped walnuts
1 teaspoon ground cinnamon
1/2 teaspoon ground nutmeg
2 cups finely chopped peeled tart apples
ICING:
1/2 cup confectioners' sugar
2-1/2 teaspoons whole milk

1 On a lightly floured surface, roll dough into a 14-in. square. Spread with butter. In a small bowl, combine the brown sugar, walnuts, cinnamon and nutmeg; add apples and toss to coat. Sprinkle over dough to within 1/2 in. of edges.

2 Roll up jelly-roll style; pinch seam to seal. Cut into 12 slices. Place cut side down in a greased 11-in. x 7-in. baking dish. Cover and let rise in a warm place until doubled, about 40 minutes.

3 Bake at 350° for 25-30 minutes or until golden brown. Combine icing ingredients until smooth; drizzle over warm rolls.

YIELD: 1 DOZEN.

when to chop

If the word "chopped" comes before an ingredient when listed in a recipe, then chop the ingredient before measuring. If the word "chopped" comes after the ingredient, then chop after measuring.

This layered corn bread "sandwich" baked in the oven is a great accompaniment for steaming soup and a salad.
Christa Habegger • Greenville, SC

ham 'n' cheddar corn bread

PREP/TOTAL TIME: 25 MIN.

2 packages (8-1/2 ounces each) corn bread/muffin mix
2/3 cup whole milk
2 eggs
1/4 pound thinly sliced deli ham
6 slices cheddar cheese

1 In a large bowl, combine the corn bread mixes, milk and eggs. Pour half of the batter into an 11-in. x 7-in. baking dish coated with cooking spray. Layer with ham and cheese; carefully spread remaining batter over the top.

2 Bake at 400° for 20-25 minutes or until a toothpick inserted near center comes out clean. Serve warm.

YIELD: 10 SERVINGS.

pull-apart bacon bread

PREP: 15 MIN. BAKE: 25 MIN.

12 bacon strips, diced

2 tubes (12 ounces each) refrigerated
   buttermilk biscuits

2 cups (8 ounces) shredded part-skim
   mozzarella cheese

1 tablespoon Italian salad dressing mix

2 teaspoons olive oil

1 In a large skillet, cook bacon over medium heat
until cooked but not crisp. Using a slotted spoon,
remove to paper towels to drain. Separate biscuits;
cut each biscuit into quarters.

2 In a large bowl, combine the cheese, dressing mix,
oil and bacon. Place half of the biscuit pieces in a
greased 10-in. fluted tube pan; sprinkle with half
of the cheese mixture. Top with remaining biscuit
pieces and cheese mixture.

3 Bake at 375° for 25-30 minutes or until golden
brown. Cool for 5 minutes before inverting onto a
serving plate. Serve immediately.

YIELD: 12 SERVINGS.

Our home economists dressed up the tops of these savory scones with fresh sage leaves. Prepared with only a handful of ingredients, the delectable wedges are ideal alongside soup, pasta or slices of oven-roasted turkey.

Taste of Home Test Kitchen

parmesan sage scones

PREP/TOTAL TIME: 25 MIN.

2-1/4 cups biscuit/baking mix
1/4 cup grated Parmesan cheese
1-3/4 teaspoons minced fresh sage
1/4 teaspoon pepper
1/2 cup plus 1 tablespoon half-and-half cream, divided
8 fresh sage leaves

1 In a large bowl, combine the biscuit mix, cheese, minced sage and pepper. Stir in 1/2 cup cream. Turn onto a floured surface; knead 5 times.

2 Transfer dough to a baking sheet coated with cooking spray. Pat into a 6-in. circle. Cut into eight wedges, but do not separate. Brush remaining cream over dough. Press a sage leave onto the top of each wedge.

3 Bake at 375° for 10-15 minutes or edges are until golden brown. Serve warm.

YIELD: 8 SCONES.

cheddar skillet corn bread

PREP/TOTAL TIME: 30 MIN.

2 tablespoons butter
2 packages (8-1/2 ounces each) corn bread/muffin mix
2 eggs, lightly beaten
1/2 cup whole milk
1/2 cup plain yogurt
1 can (14-3/4 ounces) cream-style corn
1/2 cup shredded cheddar cheese
HONEY BUTTER:
1/2 cup butter, softened
2 tablespoons honey

1 Place butter into a deep 10-in. ovenproof skillet. Place in a 400° oven for 4-6 minutes or until melted.

2 Meanwhile, in a large bowl, combine the corn bread mix, eggs, milk and yogurt until blended. Stir in corn and cheese. Pour into hot skillet.

3 Bake at 400° for 20-25 minutes or until a toothpick inserted near the center comes out clean. Cut into wedges. Cream together butter and honey. Serve with warm corn bread.

YIELD: 1 LOAF (12 WEDGES).

apricot-date mini loaves

PREP: 10 MIN. BAKE: 25 MIN. + COOLING

1 package (19.1 ounces) cinnamon swirl muffin mix
1/2 teaspoon baking powder
2 eggs, lightly beaten
2/3 cup orange juice
1/2 cup chopped dried apricots
1/2 cup chopped dates

1 Set aside cinnamon swirl and topping packets from muffin mix. In a large bowl, combine muffin mix and baking powder. Make a well in the center; add eggs and orange juice. Stir just until moistened. Fold in apricots and dates. Pour into four greased 5-in. x 3-in. x 2-in. loaf pans.

2 Squeeze contents of cinnamon swirl packet over batter; cut through with a knife to swirl. Sprinkle with the topping.

3 Bake at 350° for 25-28 minutes or until a toothpick inserted near the centers of the loaves comes out clean. Cool for 10 minutes before removing from pans to wire racks.

YIELD: 4 LOAVES (5 SLICES EACH).

deviled ham muffins

PREP/TOTAL TIME: 30 MIN.

The filling for these savory muffins is what makes them special.

Roberta Morgan • Yakima, WA

2 tablespoons finely chopped carrot
2 tablespoons finely chopped celery
2 tablespoons finely chopped onion
1 tablespoon butter
1 can (4-1/4 ounces) deviled ham spread
2 cups biscuit/baking mix
1 tablespoon sugar
1 egg
2/3 cup whole milk
1/2 cup shredded cheddar cheese

1 In a small skillet, saute the carrot, celery and onion in butter until tender. Remove from the heat; stir in ham and set aside.

2 In a large bowl, combine biscuit mix and sugar. Whisk egg and milk; stir into dry ingredients just until moistened. Fold in cheese.

3 Fill greased or paper-lined muffin cups three-fourths full. Make an indentation in the center of each muffin; fill with 1 tablespoon ham mixture.

4 Bake at 400° for 15-17 minutes or until a toothpick inserted in the center of the muffins comes out clean. Cool for 5 minutes before removing from pan to a wire rack. Serve warm.

YIELD: 10 MUFFINS.

Here's a bread recipe that is perfect for individual portions. Add them to a meal or snack on them as an appetizer.

Janice Bassing
Racine, WI

mini focaccia

PREP/TOTAL TIME: 25 MIN.

1 tube (11 ounces) refrigerated breadsticks
2 teaspoons olive oil
1 teaspoon Italian seasoning
2 tablespoons grated Parmesan cheese

1 Remove dough from tube; do not unroll breadsticks. Cut dough into eight slices. Press into 4-1/2-in. circles on greased baking sheets.

2 Brush with oil; sprinkle with Italian seasoning and cheese. Bake at 375° for 10-15 minutes or until golden brown.

YIELD: 8 FOCACCIA.

sauteing

The word "saute" is French and means to cook or lightly brown foods in butter, margarine or oil until tender. A saute pan is wide and has straight or slightly sloped sides.

buttons and bows

PREP: 20 MIN. BAKE: 10 MIN.

2 cups biscuit/baking mix
2 tablespoons plus 1/4 cup sugar, divided
1 teaspoon ground nutmeg
1/8 teaspoon ground cinnamon
1 egg
1/3 cup whole milk
1/4 cup butter, melted

1 In a large bowl, combine the biscuit mix, 2 tablespoons sugar, nutmeg and cinnamon. Combine egg and milk; stir into dry ingredients just until moistened.

2 Turn onto a heavily floured surface; knead 5-6 times. Roll out to 1/4-in. thickness. Cut with a floured 2-1/2-in. doughnut cutter; set centers aside for buttons.

3 For bows, twist each circle to form a figure eight; place on a greased baking sheet. Bake at 400° for 8-10 minutes or until golden brown.

4 Place buttons on another greased baking sheet. Bake for 6-7 minutes. Brush the tops with butter; sprinkle with remaining sugar. Remove from pans to wire racks. Serve warm.

YIELD: 1 DOZEN BUTTONS AND BOWS.

A flavorful combination of herbs makes this cheese-topped loaf a welcome addition to most any menu. In fact, we couldn't believe how light the buttery slices were when compared to frozen breads found in the grocery store.

Taste of Home Test Kitchen

herb cheese bread

PREP: 15 MIN. BAKE: 20 MIN.

1/4 cup finely chopped green onions
2 garlic cloves, minced
1/3 cup reduced-fat margarine
1/2 teaspoon ground cumin
1/4 teaspoon dried oregano
1/4 teaspoon dried thyme
1/8 teaspoon salt
1/8 teaspoon crushed red pepper flakes
1 loaf (1 pound) unsliced French bread, halved lengthwise
3/4 cup shredded reduced-fat cheddar cheese

1 In a small nonstick skillet, saute the onions and garlic in margarine for 1-2 minutes. Stir in the seasonings. Brush over the cut sides of French bread; sprinkle with cheese.

2 Wrap each piece of bread loosely in a large piece of heavy-duty foil; seal edges of foil. Bake at 400° for 20-25 minutes or until heated through and cheese is melted. Cut each piece into six slices. Serve warm.

YIELD: 12 SERVINGS.

EDITOR'S NOTE: This recipe was tested with Blue Bonnet light stick margarine.

I had been making garlic cheese biscuits for years before I tried spicing them up with some green chilies. These biscuits go well with soups as well as Mexican and Italian food.

LaDonna Reed
Ponca City, OK

italian drop biscuits

PREP/TOTAL TIME: 20 MIN.

2 cups biscuit/baking mix

1 cup (4 ounces) shredded cheddar cheese

1/2 cup cold water

2 tablespoons chopped green chilies

1/4 cup butter, melted

1 teaspoon dried parsley flakes

1/2 teaspoon Italian seasoning

1/4 teaspoon garlic powder

1 In a large bowl, combine the biscuit mix, cheddar cheese, water and chilies just until moistened. Drop by heaping tablespoonfuls onto a greased baking sheet.

2 Bake at 450° for 8-10 minutes or until golden brown. In a small bowl, combine the butter, parsley, Italian seasoning and garlic powder; brush over warm biscuits.

YIELD: 1-1/2 DOZEN.

poppy seed muffins

PREP/TOTAL TIME: 30 MIN.

3/4 cup biscuit/baking mix

1/4 cup sugar

1-1/2 teaspoons poppy seeds

1 egg

1/3 cup sour cream

1/2 teaspoon vanilla extract

1 In a large bowl, combine the biscuit mix, sugar and poppy seeds. In another bowl, whisk the egg, sour cream and vanilla; stir into dry ingredients just until moistened. Fill greased or paper-lined muffin cups two-thirds full.

2 Bake at 400° for 15-20 minutes or until a toothpick inserted near the center comes out clean. Cool for 5 minutes before removing from pan to a wire rack. Serve warm.

YIELD: 6 MUFFINS.

herbed garlic bread

PREP/TOTAL TIME: 30 MIN.

1/2 cup butter, softened

1/4 cup grated Romano cheese

2 tablespoons minced fresh basil or 2 teaspoons dried basil

1 tablespoon minced fresh parsley

3 garlic cloves, minced

1 loaf (1 pound) French bread, halved lengthwise

4 ounces provolone cheese, shredded, optional

1 In a small bowl, combine the butter, Romano cheese, basil, parsley and garlic. Spread over cut sides of bread. Sprinkle with provolone cheese if desired. Place on an ungreased baking sheet.

2 Bake at 425° for 10-12 minutes or until the cheese is melted. Slice and serve warm.

YIELD: 8 SERVINGS.

golden garlic bread

PREP/TOTAL TIME: 20 MIN.

3/4 cup butter, softened

1/2 cup mayonnaise

3 cups (12 ounces) shredded cheddar cheese

1/2 cup grated Parmesan cheese

3 green onions, chopped

1 teaspoon Italian seasoning

1 to 2 garlic cloves, minced

1 loaf (1 pound) French bread,
  cut in half lengthwise

1 In a small bowl, beat butter and mayonnaise
  until blended. Stir in the cheeses, onions, Italian
  seasoning and garlic. Spread over cut sides of
  bread. Place on an ungreased baking sheet.

2 Broil 4-6 in. from the heat for 3-5 minutes or until
  the topping is lightly browned and bubbly. Cut into
  2-in. slices.

YIELD: 4-6 SERVINGS.

swirled dill rolls

PREP/TOTAL TIME: 20 MIN.

1 tube (8 ounces) refrigerated crescent rolls
2 tablespoons butter, softened
1/4 teaspoon onion powder
1/4 teaspoon snipped fresh dill

1 Do not unroll crescent dough; cut into eight equal slices. Place cut side down on an ungreased baking sheet. Bake at 375° for 11-13 minutes or until golden brown. Meanwhile, in a small bowl, combine the butter, onion powder and dill. Spread over warm rolls.

YIELD: 8 ROLLS.

You'll need just four ingredients to bake a pan of these golden-brown rolls. With their fresh-from-the-oven aroma and mild dill flavor, they complement any ham dish nicely. Or serve the rolls with most any entree.

Taste of Home Test Kitchen

ultimate corn bread

PREP: 15 MIN. BAKE: 30 MIN. + COOLING

My corn bread recipe is out of this world. I think it's the tastiest I've ever had.

Nita Cameron • Tacoma, WA

2-1/2 cups biscuit/baking mix
1 cup sugar
2/3 cup cornmeal
1/4 teaspoon baking powder
1/4 teaspoon ground nutmeg
2 eggs
1-1/4 cups whole milk
1-1/4 cups butter, melted

1 In a large bowl, combine the first five ingredients. In another bowl, whisk the eggs, milk and butter; stir into the dry ingredients just until moistened. Pour into a greased 9-in. square baking pan.

2 Bake at 350° for 30-35 minutes or until a toothpick inserted near the center comes out clean. Cool for 15 minutes before cutting. Serve warm.

YIELD: 12 SERVINGS.

cornmeal

Cornmeal can be either white, yellow or blue depending on which strain of corn is used. Traditionally, white cornmeal is preferred in the South and yellow in the North. All three can be used interchangeably in recipes.

chocolate biscuit puffs

PREP/TOTAL TIME: 20 MIN.

1 package (7-1/2 ounces) refrigerated flaky
 buttermilk biscuits

1 milk chocolate candy bar (1.55 ounces)

2 teaspoons cinnamon-sugar

1 Flatten each biscuit into a 3-in. circle. Break candy
 bar into 10 pieces; place a piece on each biscuit.
 Bring up edges to enclose candy and pinch to seal.

2 Place on an ungreased baking sheet. Sprinkle with
 cinnamon-sugar. Bake at 450° for 8-10 minutes or
 until golden brown.

YIELD: 10 SERVINGS.

fun for kids

Chocolate Biscuit Puffs are
great for children's parties.
To add some festive flair to
them, use bright colors of
sugar to sprinkle over them.
The kids can help decorate, too!

pistachio quick bread

PREP: 20 MIN. BAKE: 35 MIN. + COOLING

I love making a few of these special loaves to give away for the holidays. The loaves also freeze well and are great to serve to unexpected guests.

Judy Fischer • Green Bay, WI

- 1 package (18-1/4 ounces) white cake mix
- 1 package (3.4 ounces) instant pistachio pudding mix
- 4 eggs
- 1 cup (8 ounces) sour cream
- 1/4 cup water
- 1/4 cup canola oil
- 1/3 cup sugar
- 3/4 teaspoon ground cinnamon

1 In a large bowl, combine cake and pudding mixes. Add the eggs, sour cream, water and oil; beat until blended (batter will be thick).

2 Combine sugar and cinnamon. Spoon half of the batter into two greased 8-in. x 4-in. loaf pans; sprinkle each with 2 tablespoons cinnamon-sugar. Spread with remaining batter; sprinkle with the remaining cinnamon-sugar.

3 Bake the loaves at 350° for 35-40 minutes or until a toothpick inserted near the centers comes out clean. Cool for 10 minutes before removing from pans to wire racks.

YIELD: 2 LOAVES (12 SLICES EACH).

You only need four ingredients to make these flavorful bread slices that are perfect for an appetizer or as a side to any pasta dish.

Margaret Wampler
Butler, PA

herbed bread slices

PREP/TOTAL TIME: 10 MIN.

- 3 tablespoons prepared Italian salad dressing
- 1 loaf (8 ounces) French bread, halved lengthwise
- 1 teaspoon dried rosemary, crushed
- 1/2 teaspoon dried oregano

1 Brush salad dressing over cut sides of bread. Sprinkle with rosemary and oregano. Place on an ungreased baking sheet. Broil 6 in. from the heat for 2-3 minutes or until lightly browned. Cut into 2-in. slices.

YIELD: 8 SERVINGS.

A soothing bowl of soup can help chase away the winter chills or be a bowl of pure comfort after a long, hard day.

sensational soups

easy seafood bisque

PREP/TOTAL TIME: 30 MIN.

1/2 cup chopped onion

1 tablespoon butter

2-1/4 cups milk

1 can (10-3/4 ounces) condensed cream of celery soup, undiluted

1 can (10-3/4 ounces) condensed cream of shrimp soup, undiluted

1 package (8 ounces) imitation crabmeat, chopped

1 teaspoon chicken bouillon granules

1/2 teaspoon dried parsley flakes

1/4 teaspoon garlic powder

1/4 teaspoon dried marjoram

1/4 teaspoon pepper

1 In a 3-qt. saucepan, saute onion in butter until tender. Stir in remaining ingredients. Cover and cook over medium-low heat for 20 minutes or until heated through, stirring occasionally.

YIELD: 4-5 SERVINGS.

soup garnishes
Dress up a soup with a sprinkle of nuts, chopped fresh herbs, sliced green onions, slivers of fresh vegetables, croutons, shredded cheese or crumbled bacon.

beer cheese soup

PREP/TOTAL TIME: 20 MIN.

2 tablespoons finely chopped onion

1/2 teaspoon butter

2 cans (10-3/4 ounces each) condensed cream of celery soup, undiluted

1 cup beer or nonalcoholic beer

1 cup whole milk

1 teaspoon Worcestershire sauce

1/2 teaspoon dried parsley flakes

1/4 teaspoon paprika

3/4 pound process cheese (Velveeta), cubed

1 In a large saucepan, saute onion in butter. Stir in the soup, beer, milk, Worcestershire sauce, parsley and paprika. Reduce heat; stir in cheese until melted. Heat through (do not boil).

YIELD: 6 SERVINGS.

ham 'n' corn chowder

PREP/TOTAL TIME: 10 MIN.

This soup comes together faster than you can believe! My family had a hard time finding a corn chowder we all liked, so I took ingredients from those we enjoyed and this is the result.

Danna Chambers • Topsham, MA

1 can (14-1/2 ounces) diced new potatoes, drained

1-1/2 cups whole milk

1 can (10-3/4 ounces) condensed cheddar cheese soup, undiluted

1 can (8-3/4 ounces) cream-style corn

1 cup frozen corn, thawed

1 cup cubed deli ham

1 In a large microwave-safe bowl, combine all the ingredients. Cover and microwave on high for 5-8 minutes or until heated through, stirring twice.

YIELD: 3 SERVINGS.

rustic italian tortellini soup

PREP: 20 MIN. COOK: 20 MIN.

3 Italian turkey sausage links (4 ounces each), casings removed

1 medium onion, chopped

6 garlic cloves, minced

2 cans (14-1/2 ounces each) reduced-sodium chicken broth

1-3/4 cups water

1 can (14-1/2 ounces) diced tomatoes, undrained

1 package (9 ounces) refrigerated cheese tortellini

1 package (6 ounces) fresh baby spinach, coarsely chopped

2-1/4 teaspoons minced fresh basil or 3/4 teaspoon dried basil

1/4 teaspoon pepper

Dash crushed red pepper flakes

Shredded Parmesan cheese, optional

1 Crumble sausage into a Dutch oven; add onion. Cook and stir over medium heat until meat is no longer pink. Add garlic; cook and stir 2 minutes longer. Add the broth, water and tomatoes. Bring to a boil.

2 Stir in tortellini; return to a boil. Cook for 7-9 minutes or until tender, stirring occasionally. Reduce heat; add the spinach, basil, pepper and pepper flakes. Cook 2-3 minutes longer or until spinach is wilted. Serve with cheese if desired.

YIELD: 6 SERVINGS (2 QUARTS).

raspberry-cranberry soup

PREP: 25 MIN. COOK: 10 MIN.

Served hot, this beautiful tangy soup helps beat the winter "blahs." On a sunny summer day, it's refreshingly cold. I have fun serving it because people are so intrigued with the idea of a fruit soup. Even doubters scrape their bowls clean.

Susan Stull • Chillicothe, MO

2 cups fresh or frozen cranberries

2 cups unsweetened apple juice

1 cup fresh or frozen unsweetened raspberries, thawed

1/2 to 1 cup sugar

1 tablespoon lemon juice

1/4 teaspoon ground cinnamon

1 tablespoon cornstarch

2 cups half-and-half cream

Whipped cream, additional raspberries and mint, optional

1 In a large saucepan, bring cranberries and apple juice to a boil. Reduce heat and simmer, uncovered, for 10 minutes. Press through a sieve; return to the pan.

2 Press the raspberries through the sieve and discard the skins and seeds. Add to the cranberry mixture; bring to a boil. Add sugar, lemon juice and cinnamon; remove from the heat.

3 Cool for 4 minutes. Combine the cornstarch and cream until smooth; gradually stir into the pan. Bring to a gentle boil; cook and stir for 2 minutes or until thickened. Serve hot or chilled. Serve with whipped cream, raspberries and mint if desired.

YIELD: 4 SERVINGS.

I need just a few canned goods to stir up this comforting microwave mixture. I call this "Throw-Together Soup." Serve it with a green salad and hot bread or rolls. You can also simmer this soup in a slow cooker.

Loellen Holley • Topock, AZ

beef soup in a hurry

PREP/TOTAL TIME: 10 MIN.

1 can (24 ounces) beef stew

1 can (14-1/2 ounces) stewed tomatoes, cut up

1 can (10-3/4 ounces) condensed vegetable beef soup, undiluted

1 can (8-3/4 ounces) whole kernel corn, drained

1/8 teaspoon hot pepper sauce

1 Combine all ingredients in a microwave-safe bowl. Cover and microwave on high for 2-3 minutes or until heated through, stirring once.

YIELD: 6 SERVINGS.

EDITOR'S NOTE: This recipe was tested in a 1,100-watt microwave.

I created my own, easy-to-prepare bean soup based on one we liked at a local Mexican restaurant. I added dumplings to make it a complete meal.

Shannon Kohn
Simpsonville, SC

bean soup with cheddar cornmeal dumplings

PREP/TOTAL TIME: 30 MIN.

1/4 cup chopped onion

1/4 cup fresh baby carrots, cut into 1/4-inch slices

1 can (15 ounces) pinto beans, rinsed and drained

1 cup chicken broth

1 cup chunky salsa

1/3 cup self-rising flour

2 tablespoons cornmeal

1/8 teaspoon salt

1/4 cup 2% milk

2 tablespoons shredded cheddar cheese

1 In a large saucepan coated with cooking spray, saute onion and carrots until tender. Stir in the beans, broth and salsa. Bring to a boil. Reduce heat; simmer, uncovered, for 3-5 minutes or until reduced slightly.

2 For the dumplings, in a small bowl, combine the flour, cornmeal and salt. Stir in milk and cheese just until moistened. Drop by tablespoonfuls onto simmering soup.

3 Cover and simmer for 15 minutes or until a toothpick inserted near the center of a dumpling comes out clean. Do not lift the cover while the soup is simmering.

YIELD: 2 SERVINGS.

EDITOR'S NOTE: As a substitute for 1/3 cup of self-rising flour, place 1/2 teaspoon baking powder and 1/8 teaspoon salt in a measuring cup. Add all-purpose flour to measure 1/3 cup.

speedy spud soup

PREP: 5 MIN. COOK: 30 MIN.

- 1 package (24 ounces) frozen shredded hash brown potatoes, thawed
- 1/2 cup chopped onion
- 1/2 cup butter, cubed
- 4 cups whole milk
- 1 can (10-3/4 ounces) condensed cream of chicken soup, undiluted
- 1 cup (4 ounces) shredded cheddar cheese
- 1/2 teaspoon garlic salt
- Cooked crumbled bacon

1 In a large saucepan, cook and stir the potatoes and onion in butter over medium-low heat for 10 minutes. Stir in the milk, soup, cheese and garlic salt. Cook, uncovered, for 20 minutes or until potatoes are tender. Garnish with bacon.

YIELD: 8 SERVINGS (2 QUARTS).

creamy wild rice soup

PREP/TOTAL TIME: 20 MIN.

Here's a quick way to add homemade appeal to canned soup and give dinner a comforting touch. It is thick and creamy with added texture from crunchy wild rice and a smoky bacon flavor.

Joanne Eickhoff • Pequot Lakes, MN

- 1/2 cup water
- 4-1/2 teaspoons dried minced onion
- 2/3 cup condensed cream of potato soup, undiluted
- 1/2 cup shredded Swiss cheese
- 1/2 cup cooked wild rice
- 1/2 cup half-and-half cream
- 2 bacon strips, cooked and crumbled

1 In a small saucepan, bring water and onion to a boil. Reduce heat. Stir in the potato soup, cheese, rice and cream; heat through (do not boil). Garnish with bacon.

YIELD: 2 SERVINGS.

cream of broccoli soup

PREP/TOTAL TIME: 25 MIN.

2 cups water

4 teaspoons chicken bouillon granules

6 cups frozen chopped broccoli

2 tablespoons finely chopped onion

2 cans (10-3/4 ounces each) condensed cream of chicken soup, undiluted

2 cups evaporated milk

2 cups (16 ounces) sour cream

1 teaspoon dried parsley flakes

1/4 teaspoon pepper

1 In a large saucepan, combine water and bouillon. Add broccoli and onion. Bring to a boil; reduce heat. Simmer for 10 minutes or until broccoli is crisp-tender.

2 In a large bowl, combine the soup, milk, sour cream, parsley and pepper; add to broccoli mixture. Cook and stir for 3-5 minutes or until heated through.

YIELD: 6-8 SERVINGS.

every last drop

Leftover evaporated milk should be transferred from the can to another container for storage. If stored in a covered container in the refrigerator, it can be used safely within 3 days.

pasta beef soup

PREP/TOTAL TIME: 25 MIN.

- 1 pound lean ground beef (90% lean)
- 2 cans (14-1/2 ounces each) beef broth
- 1 package (16 ounces) frozen pasta with broccoli, corn and carrots in garlic-seasoned sauce
- 1-1/2 cups tomato juice
- 1 can (14-1/2 ounces) diced tomatoes, undrained
- 2 teaspoons Italian seasoning
- 1/4 cup shredded Parmesan cheese, optional

1 In a large saucepan, cook beef over medium heat until no longer pink; drain. Add the broth, pasta with vegetables, tomato juice, tomatoes and Italian seasoning; bring to a boil. Reduce heat; cover and simmer for 10 minutes or until vegetables are tender. Serve with cheese if desired.

YIELD: 6 SERVINGS.

This tasty soup can be prepared in no time. Handy canned goods, tomato juice and frozen pasta-vegetable medley make this recipe flavorful and fast.

Brenda Jackson
Garden City, KS

cannellini comfort soup

PREP: 15 MIN. COOK: 35 MIN.

Reduced-fat sausage, white beans and veggies make this nutritious soup plenty filling. Plus, it warms you from head to toe. If you are feeling creative, try adding some chopped fresh carrots along with onion and pepper...or more chicken broth for a "soupier" effect.

Susan Coryell • Huddleston, VA

- 1/2 pound reduced-fat fully cooked smoked sausage, cut into bite-size pieces
- 1 tablespoon olive oil
- 1/2 cup chopped green pepper
- 1/3 cup chopped onion
- 2 garlic cloves, minced
- 1 can (14-1/2 ounces) reduced-sodium chicken broth
- 1/3 cup white wine or chicken broth
- 1/2 teaspoon Italian seasoning
- 1/4 teaspoon pepper
- 1 can (15 ounces) white kidney or cannellini beans, rinsed and drained
- 3 cups coleslaw mix

1 In a large saucepan, cook sausage in oil for 2 minutes. Add green pepper and onion. Cook and stir 2-3 minutes or until vegetables are tender. Add garlic: cook 1 minute longer.

2 Stir in the broth, wine, Italian seasoning and pepper. Bring to a boil. Reduce the heat; cover and simmer for 15 minutes.

3 Stir in beans and coleslaw mix. Return to a boil. Reduce heat; cover and simmer until beans are heated through and cabbage is tender.

YIELD: 4 SERVINGS.

tomato florentine soup

PREP: 40 MIN. COOK: 25 MIN.

When I get a craving for this soup in summer, I head outside and pick garden-fresh tomatoes and basil. Use whatever kind of pasta you have on hand.

Engracia Salley • Bristol, RI

4 garlic cloves, minced

3 tablespoons olive oil

8 medium tomatoes, chopped

4 cups spicy hot V8 vegetable juice

3/4 cup uncooked small pasta shells

1/2 teaspoon salt

1/8 teaspoon pepper

1 package (10 ounces) fresh baby spinach

3 tablespoons minced fresh basil or 1 tablespoon dried basil

1 In a large saucepan, saute garlic in oil for 1 minute. Add tomatoes; cook and stir for 5-10 minutes or until tender. Add the vegetable juice, pasta, salt and pepper; bring to a boil. Reduce heat; cover and simmer for 20-25 minutes or until pasta is tender.

2 Stir in the spinach and basil. Cook 5 minutes longer or until spinach is wilted.

YIELD: 9 SERVINGS.

Since my husband and I both work full-time, it's nice to have a winter pick-me-up like this zippy favorite to call on when I need a speedy and filling entree for supper.

Carole Holder • Norman, OK

taco minestrone

PREP/TOTAL TIME: 25 MIN.

1/2 pound ground beef

2 cans (15 ounces each) Ranch Style beans (pinto beans in seasoned tomato sauce)

2 cans (10-3/4 ounces each) condensed minestrone soup, undiluted

2 cans (10 ounces each) diced tomatoes and green chilies, undrained

1 In a large saucepan, cook beef over medium heat until no longer pink; drain. Stir in the beans, soup and tomatoes. Bring to a boil. Reduce heat; simmer, uncovered for 15-20 minutes.

YIELD: 8 SERVINGS.

tomato tip

The best way to cut through the skin of a tomato is with a serrated, not straight-edged, knife. Cut vertically, from stem end to blossom end, for slices that will be less juicy and hold their shape better.

My rich and satisfying chowder took top prize at a recipe competition. This family favorite is perhaps the easiest recipe for clam chowder that I have ever made. It's especially delicious when served with sourdough bread!

Lori Kimble
McDonald, PA

creamy clam chowder

PREP: 15 MIN. COOK: 30 MIN.

1 large onion, chopped

3 medium carrots, chopped

2 celery ribs, sliced

3/4 cup butter, cubed

2 cans (10-3/4 ounces each) condensed cream of potato soup, undiluted

3 cans (6-1/2 ounces each) minced clams

3 tablespoons cornstarch

1 quart half-and-half cream

1 In a large saucepan, saute the onion, carrots and celery in butter until tender. Stir in the potato soup and two cans of the undrained clams. Drain and discard the juice from the remaining can of clams; add clams to soup.

2 Combine cornstarch and a small amount of cream until smooth; stir into soup. Add the remaining cream. Bring to a boil; cook and stir for 2 minutes or until thickened.

YIELD: 9 SERVINGS (ABOUT 2 QUARTS).

pumpkin soup

PREP/TOTAL TIME: 20 MIN.

1/2 cup finely chopped onion

2 tablespoons butter

1 tablespoon all-purpose flour

2 cans (14-1/2 ounces each) chicken broth

1 can (15 ounces) solid-pack pumpkin

1 teaspoon brown sugar

1/4 teaspoon salt

1/8 teaspoon pepper

1/8 teaspoon ground nutmeg

1 cup heavy whipping cream

1 In a large saucepan, saute onion in butter until tender. Remove from the heat; stir in flour until blended. Gradually stir in broth, pumpkin, brown sugar, salt, pepper and nutmeg; bring to a boil. Reduce heat and simmer for 5 minutes. Add cream; cook for 2 minutes or until heated through.

YIELD: 6 SERVINGS.

white chili

PREP/TOTAL TIME: 10 MIN.

This recipe went from a great mistake to a tasty triumph. I created it accidentally, and it got rave reviews. Now I whip up the quick-as-lightning dish when I'm pinched for time.

Cynthia Lynn Bloemker • Effingham, IL

1 jar (48 ounces) great northern beans, rinsed and drained

2 cans (one 10 ounces, one 5 ounces) chunk white chicken, drained

1-1/4 cups whole milk

1 cup (8 ounces) sour cream

1 can (4 ounces) chopped green chilies

1 teaspoon salt-free seasoning blend

1 cup (4 ounces) shredded Italian cheese blend

2 tablespoons minced fresh cilantro

Additional sour cream, optional

1 In a large saucepan, combine the first six ingredients. Bring to a boil over medium-high heat; remove from the heat. Add cheese and cilantro; stir until cheese is melted. Garnish with additional sour cream if desired.

YIELD: 8 SERVINGS (2 QUARTS).

cheeseburger soup

PREP/TOTAL TIME: 30 MIN.

1 cup shredded carrot

1 cup chopped onion

1/2 cup chopped celery

2 cans (14-1/2 ounces each) chicken broth

1 pound ground beef, cooked, crumbled and drained

2 cups cooked long grain rice

3 cups milk

1 pound process cheese (Velveeta), cubed

1 cup (8 ounces) sour cream

1 In a large saucepan, combine the carrot, onion, celery and broth. Bring to a boil. Reduce heat; simmer, uncovered, for 15 minutes or until vegetables are tender.

2 Stir in the beef, rice, milk and cheese; simmer, uncovered, until cheese is melted, stirring occasionally (do not boil). Just before serving, whisk in the sour cream; heat through.

YIELD: 10 SERVINGS (ABOUT 2-1/2 QUARTS).

stroganoff soup

PREP: 15 MIN. COOK: 40 MIN.

My husband and I share a love for all kinds of soup and created this delicious recipe together. It tastes just like beef Stroganoff. With a crusty roll, it's a hearty meal.

Karen Shiveley • Springfield, MN

1/2 pound beef top sirloin steak or beef tenderloin, cut into thin strips

1/2 cup chopped onion

1 tablespoon butter

2 cups water

1-1/2 cups milk

1/4 cup tomato paste

2 teaspoons beef bouillon granules

1 can (8 ounces) mushroom stems and pieces, drained

1 teaspoon salt

1/8 teaspoon pepper

1 can (12 ounces) evaporated milk

1/3 cup all-purpose flour

2 cups cooked wide egg noodles

1/2 cup sour cream

1 In a 3-qt. saucepan, cook beef and onion in butter over medium heat, until meat is browned. Stir in the water, milk, tomato paste and bouillon. Add mushrooms, salt and pepper; bring to a boil. Reduce heat; cover and simmer for 20-30 minutes or until meat is tender.

2 Combine evaporated milk and flour until smooth. Gradually add to soup. Bring to a boil; cook and stir for 2 minutes until thickened. Add noodles; cook until heated through. Remove from the heat; stir in sour cream.

YIELD: 6 SERVINGS.

Here's an easy way to jazz up canned soup. I created the recipe after eating tangy tomato soup in a restaurant. After a few tries, I came up with this version. It is so simple and very satisfying.

Chris Christopher
Albuquerque, NM

green chili tomato soup

PREP/TOTAL TIME: 10 MIN.

1 can (10-3/4 ounces) condensed tomato soup, undiluted

3/4 cup whole milk

1 can (4 ounces) chopped green chilies

1/2 cup shredded cheddar cheese

1 In a small saucepan, combine the soup, milk and chilies until blended. Cook and stir over medium heat until heated through. Sprinkle with cheese.

YIELD: 2 SERVINGS.

This chowder is like a bacon-topped baked potato in a bowl. On cold winter days, my family is thrilled to see it on the table.

Jacque Manning
Burbank, CA

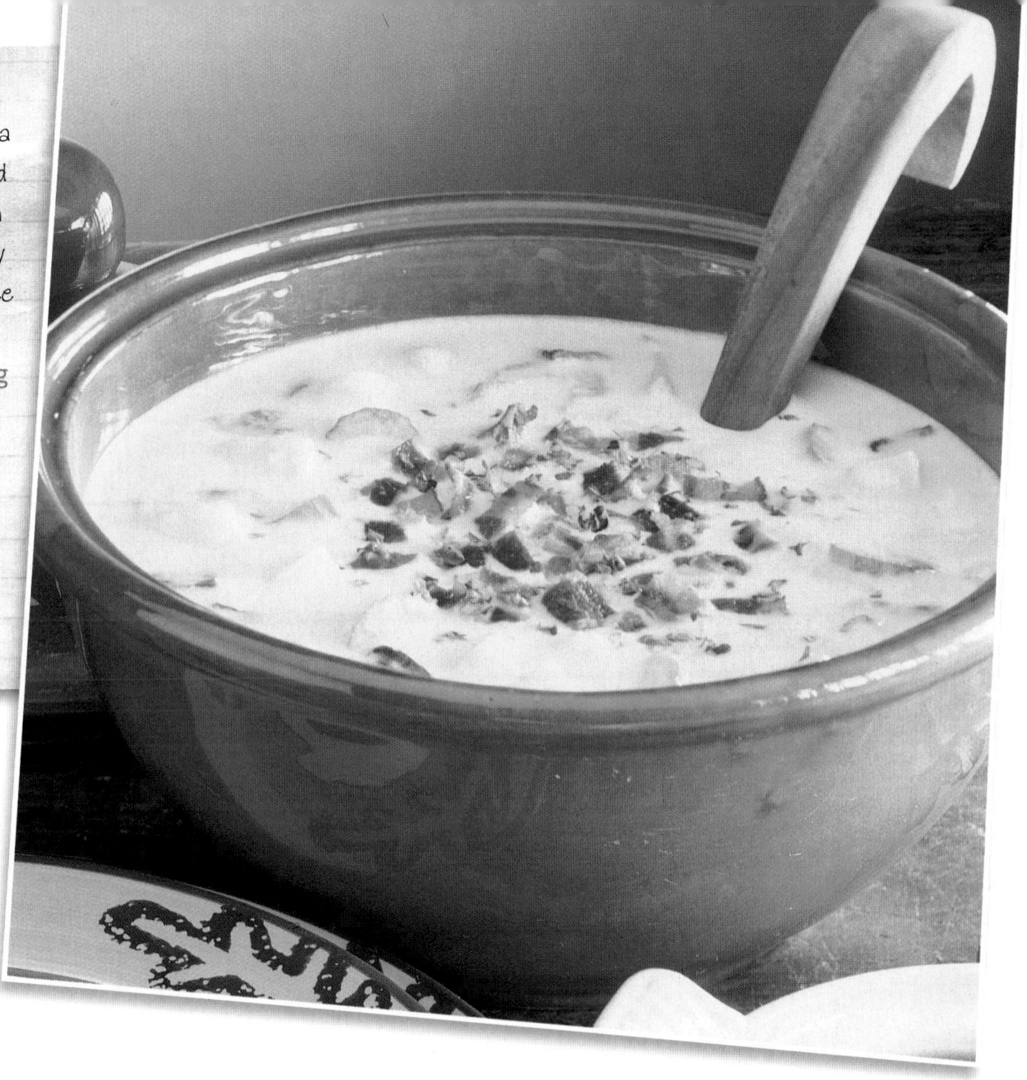

potato bacon chowder

PREP/TOTAL TIME: 30 MIN.

- 2 cups cubed peeled potatoes
- 1 cup water
- 8 bacon strips
- 1 cup chopped onion
- 1/2 cup chopped celery
- 1 can (10-3/4 ounces) condensed cream of chicken soup, undiluted
- 1-3/4 cups whole milk
- 1 cup (8 ounces) sour cream
- 1/2 teaspoon salt
- Dash pepper
- 1 tablespoon minced fresh parsley

1 Place potatoes in a small saucepan and cover with water. Bring to a boil. Reduce heat; cover and cook for 10-15 minutes or until tender.

2 Meanwhile, in a large skillet, cook bacon until crisp; remove to paper towels to drain and set aside.

3 In the same skillet, saute onion and celery in drippings until tender; drain. Add to undrained potatoes. Stir in the soup, milk, sour cream, salt and pepper. Cook over low heat for 10 minutes or until heated through (do not boil).

4 Crumble bacon; set aside 1/4 cup. Add remaining bacon to soup along with parsley. Sprinkle with reserved bacon.

YIELD: 6 SERVINGS.

fish chowder

PREP/TOTAL TIME: 30 MIN.

1 bacon strip, diced

2 tablespoons chopped onion

2 tablespoons chopped celery

2/3 cup condensed cream of
   potato soup, undiluted

1/2 cup water

1/8 teaspoon pepper

Dash salt

1/2 pound haddock fillets, cut into 1-inch pieces

1/2 cup whole milk

1-1/2 teaspoons butter

Oyster crackers, optional

1 In a small saucepan, saute the bacon, onion and celery until the vegetables are tender. Add the soup, water, pepper and salt. Bring to a boil; reduce heat.

2 Add haddock; cover and simmer for 8-12 minutes or until fish flakes easily with a fork. Stir in the milk and butter; heat through. Serve with oyster crackers if desired.

YIELD: 2 SERVINGS.

pesto minestrone

PREP/TOTAL TIME: 30 MIN.

1/2 cup chopped onion
2 teaspoons olive oil
1 teaspoon minced garlic
2-1/4 cups water
2 cups frozen mixed vegetables
1 can (14-1/2 ounces) vegetable broth
3/4 teaspoon dried oregano
1/2 teaspoon salt
1/2 teaspoon pepper
1 package (9 ounces) refrigerated cheese tortellini
2 cups diced zucchini
2 tablespoons prepared pesto

1 In a large saucepan, saute onion in oil until tender. Add garlic; cook 1 minute longer. Stir in the water, mixed vegetables, broth, oregano, salt and pepper. Bring to a boil. Reduce heat; cover and simmer for 3 minutes.

2 Add the tortellini, zucchini and pesto. Simmer, uncovered, 7-9 minutes longer or until pasta and vegetables are tender.

YIELD: 4 SERVINGS.

I rely on store-bought pesto to provide mild flavor to chunky tortellini and vegetable soup. It's a hit in my house. If you don't like zucchini, use another green vegetable, such as asparagus or green beans.

Natalie Cataldo
Des Moines, IA

potato soup in bread bowls

PREP/TOTAL TIME: 20 MIN.

This heartwarming main course helps my husband get a swift yet satisfying meal on the table when I'm at work. He loves clam chowder and my simple recipe lets him prepare it in just minutes.

Cheryl Cor • Auburn, WA

2 cans (18.8 ounces each) ready-to-serve chunky baked potato with cheddar and bacon bits soup
2 cans (6-1/2 ounces each) chopped clams, drained
1 bacon strip, cooked and crumbled
1 teaspoon minced chives
1 teaspoon dried parsley flakes
1 teaspoon dried rosemary, crushed
1/4 teaspoon pepper
5 round loaves (8 ounces each) sourdough bread

1 In a large saucepan, combine the potato soup, clams, bacon, chives, parsley, rosemary and pepper; heat through.

2 Meanwhile, cut a thin slice off the top of each loaf of sourdough bread and set aside. Hollow out the loaves, leaving a 3/4-in. shell for each loaf (discard the removed bread or save it for another use). Ladle the finished soup into the bread bowls and replace the tops.

YIELD: 5 SERVINGS.

Every scrumptious meal in this chapter comes together in a snap...many need just 20 minutes of prep work or less!

memorable
main courses

Grilled pork chops have a lovely stuffing of couscous, cherries and seasonings in this quick and elegant main dish. Served with a salad, it's perfect for special occasions, but speedy enough for everyday family suppers.

Taste of Home
Test Kitchen

cherry-stuffed pork chops

PREP: 20 MIN. GRILL: 20 MIN.

1 package (5.6 ounces) couscous with toasted pine nuts

6 boneless pork loin chops (1 inch thick and 6 ounces each)

1/2 cup dried cherries

1 tablespoon brown sugar

1 tablespoon butter, melted

1/2 teaspoon minced fresh gingerroot

1/2 teaspoon garlic powder

1/2 teaspoon pepper

1 Prepare couscous according to package directions. Meanwhile, cut a deep slit in each pork chop, forming a pocket. Stir the cherries, brown sugar, butter and ginger into prepared couscous. Stuff 1/3 cup into each chop; secure with toothpicks. Sprinkle with garlic powder and pepper.

2 Grill pork chops, covered, over medium heat for 10-12 minutes on each side or until a meat thermometer reads 160°. Discard toothpicks.

YIELD: 6 SERVINGS.

shrimp kabobs

PREP: 35 MIN. + MARINATING GRILL: 10 MIN.

1 cup Italian salad dressing, divided
2 pounds uncooked jumbo shrimp, peeled and deveined
2 large onions
16 large fresh mushrooms
2 large green peppers, cut into 1-1/2-inch pieces
16 cherry tomatoes

1 In a large resealable plastic bag, combine 1/2 cup salad dressing and shrimp. Cut each onion into eight wedges. In another large resealable plastic bag, combine the vegetables and remaining dressing. Seal bags and turn to coat. Refrigerate for 2 hours, turning occasionally.

2 Drain and discard marinade. On eight metal or soaked wooden skewers, alternately thread the shrimp and vegetables. Grill kabobs, covered, over medium heat or broil 4 in. from the heat for 6 minutes or until shrimp turn pink, turning occasionally.

YIELD: 8 SERVINGS.

chicken noodle delight

PREP: 25 MIN. BAKE: 35 MIN.

This recipe is comfort food at its finest. Although it's perfect for fall or winter, the creamy casserole makes any day better!

Gail Schumacher • Berthoud, CO

4 cups uncooked egg noodles

1 can (10-3/4 ounces) condensed cream of chicken soup, undiluted

1 package (8 ounces) cream cheese, cubed

1 cup (8 ounces) sour cream

1/4 cup whole milk

3 tablespoons minced fresh parsley or 1 tablespoon dried parsley flakes

1 teaspoon salt

1 teaspoon onion salt

2 cups cubed cooked chicken

1-1/4 cups crushed saltines (about 35 crackers)

1/2 cup butter, melted

1 Cook noodles according to package directions. Meanwhile, in a large bowl, combine the soup, cream cheese, sour cream, milk, parsley, salt and onion salt. Stir in chicken.

2 Drain noodles; toss with chicken mixture. Transfer to a greased 2-qt. baking dish.

3 Combine the cracker crumbs and butter; sprinkle over the casserole. Bake, uncovered, at 350° for 35-40 minutes or until golden brown.

YIELD: 6 SERVINGS.

Here, chive and onion cream cheese and a few other on-hand items make a delicious sauce for baked pork chops.

Taste of Home
Test Kitchen

breaded pork chops

PREP/TOTAL TIME: 30 MIN.

1 egg

3/4 cup seasoned bread crumbs

4 bone-in pork loin chops (1/2 inch thick and 6 ounces each)

1 carton (8 ounces) spreadable chive and onion cream cheese

3 tablespoons chicken broth

2 tablespoons whole milk

1 In a shallow bowl, beat the egg. Place the bread crumbs in another shallow bowl. Dip pork chops into egg, then coat with crumbs. Place in a greased 15-in. x 10-in. x 1-in. baking pan. Bake, uncovered, at 350° for 25-30 minutes or until a meat thermometer reads 160°.

2 In a small saucepan, combine the cream cheese, broth and milk. Cook and stir over medium heat for 5 minutes or until smooth and blended. Serve with pork chops.

YIELD: 4 SERVINGS.

My friends shared this recipe with me, and my whole family really enjoys it. I like that it's so tasty and quick to prepare.

Danelle Weiher
Verndale, MN

salisbury steak with gravy

PREP: 15 MIN. BAKE: 50 MIN.

1/2 cup fat-free milk

14 fat-free saltines, crushed

2 tablespoons dried minced onion

2 teaspoons dried parsley flakes

1 pound lean ground beef (90% lean)

1 jar (12 ounces) fat-free beef gravy

2 tablespoons ketchup

2 teaspoons Worcestershire sauce

1/4 teaspoon pepper

1 In a large bowl, combine the milk, saltines, onion and parsley. Crumble beef over mixture and mix well. Shape into four patties. Place in an 8-in. square baking dish coated with cooking spray.

2 In a small bowl, combine the gravy, ketchup, Worcestershire and pepper; pour over patties. Bake, uncovered, at 350° for 50-55 minutes or until a meat thermometer reads 160°.

YIELD: 4 SERVINGS.

super sauce

Worcestershire sauce is made of soy sauce, vinegar, garlic, onions, tamarind, molasses and various seasonings. It's widely available in supermarkets.

teriyaki beef tenderloin

PREP: 10 MIN. + MARINATING
BAKE: 45 MIN. + STANDING

1 cup sherry or reduced-sodium beef broth
1/2 cup reduced-sodium soy sauce
1 envelope onion soup mix
1/4 cup packed brown sugar
1 beef tenderloin roast (2 pounds)
2 tablespoons water

1 In a large bowl, combine the sherry, soy sauce, soup mix and brown sugar. Pour 1 cup into a large resealable plastic bag; add tenderloin. Seal bag and turn to coat; refrigerate for 5 hours or overnight. Cover and refrigerate remaining marinade.

2 Drain and discard marinade. Place tenderloin on a rack in a shallow roasting pan. Bake, uncovered, at 425° for 45-50 minutes or until meat reaches desired doneness (for medium-rare, a meat thermometer should read 145°; medium, 160°; well-done, 170°), basting often with 1/3 cup reserved marinade. Let stand for 10-15 minutes.

3 Meanwhile, in a small saucepan, bring water and remaining marinade to a rolling boil for 1 minute or until sauce is slightly reduced. Slice the beef and serve with the sauce.

YIELD: 8 SERVINGS.

chicken coleslaw wraps

PREP/TOTAL TIME: 20 MIN.

1 pound boneless skinless chicken breasts,
   cut into 1-inch strips

1/4 teaspoon salt

1/8 teaspoon pepper

1 tablespoon canola oil

1-1/2 cups deli coleslaw

1/2 cup pineapple tidbits

4 sun-dried tomato tortillas (10 inches), warmed

1 medium tomato, sliced

1 cup (4 ounces) shredded cheddar cheese

1 Sprinkle the chicken with salt and pepper. In a large
  skillet, cook chicken in oil over medium heat for
  10-15 minutes or until no longer pink.

2 Combine coleslaw and pineapple; spread evenly over
  each tortilla. Layer with tomato, cheese and chicken;
  roll up tightly.

YIELD: 4 SERVINGS.

Convenient deli coleslaw, chicken and other
easy-to-find ingredients create tasty wraps,
which make a lovely summer lunch.
Taste of Home Test Kitchen

saucy mushroom pork chops

PREP/TOTAL TIME: 30 MIN.

*I came up with an easy way to dress up ordinary pork chops. My
husband loves them, and the rich and creamy sauce tastes great
over mashed potatoes.*

Karlene Lantz • Felton, CA

6 boneless pork loin chops (4 ounces each)

1/4 teaspoon salt

1/4 teaspoon pepper

2 teaspoons olive oil, divided

1 cup sliced fresh mushrooms

1/3 cup chopped onion

1 garlic clove, minced

1/2 cup white wine or reduced-sodium
  chicken broth

1 can (10-3/4 ounces) reduced-fat reduced-
  sodium condensed cream of mushroom
  soup, undiluted

1/2 cup reduced-sodium chicken broth

1 Sprinkle the pork chops with salt and pepper. In a
  large nonstick skillet, brown chops on both sides in
  1 teaspoon oil; remove and keep warm. In the same
  skillet, saute the mushrooms, onion and garlic in
  remaining oil until tender.

2 Add wine or broth, stirring up any browned bits;
  cook for 4-6 minutes or until liquid is reduced by half.
  Stir in soup and broth. Bring to a boil. Return pork
  chops to the pan. Reduce heat; simmer, uncovered,
  for 8-10 minutes or until meat juices run clear.

YIELD: 6 SERVINGS.

pear chutney chicken

PREP/TOTAL TIME: 30 MIN.

1 can (15-1/4 ounces) sliced pears

4 boneless skinless chicken breast halves (4 ounces each)

2 tablespoons all-purpose flour

1/4 teaspoon pepper

2 tablespoons olive oil

1/2 cup chopped onion

1/2 cup mango chutney

1 to 2 tablespoons lemon juice

3/4 to 1 teaspoon curry powder

1 Drain pears, reserving 1/4 cup juice; set pears and juice aside. Flatten chicken to 1/4-in. thickness. In a large resealable bag, combine flour and pepper. Add chicken in batches and shake to coat.

2 In a large skillet, cook chicken in oil over medium heat for 5-6 minutes on each side or until a meat thermometer reads 170°. Remove and keep warm.

3 In the same skillet, combine the onion, chutney, lemon juice, curry powder and reserved pear juice. Bring to a boil. Add chicken and pears. Reduce heat; simmer, uncovered, for 3-5 minutes or until heated through.

YIELD: 4 SERVINGS.

open-faced reubens

PREP/TOTAL TIME: 20 MIN.

2-1/2 cups coleslaw mix

8 green onions, sliced

1/2 cup mayonnaise, divided

2 tablespoons cider vinegar

1/2 teaspoon salt

1/2 teaspoon pepper

1/4 cup Dijon mustard

8 slices rye bread, lightly toasted

16 slices Swiss cheese

1 pound thinly sliced deli corned beef

1 In a large bowl, combine the coleslaw mix, onions, 1/4 cup mayonnaise, vinegar, salt and pepper. Cover and refrigerate until chilled.

2 Meanwhile, combine the Dijon mustard and the remaining mayonnaise. Spread over one side of each slice of toast; top with a cheese slice, corned beef and another cheese slice. Place on foil-lined baking sheets.

3 Bake at 450° for 5-6 minutes or until cheese is melted. Top each with 1/4 cup coleslaw.

YIELD: 8 SERVINGS.

easy haddock bake

PREP: 15 MIN. BAKE: 25 MIN.

2 pounds haddock fillets

1 can (10-3/4 ounces) condensed cream of shrimp soup, undiluted

2 tablespoons lemon juice

2 tablespoons sherry or reduced-sodium chicken broth

2 tablespoons finely chopped onion

4-1/2 teaspoons butter

2 garlic cloves, minced

1/4 cup dry bread crumbs

1/4 teaspoon Worcestershire sauce

1 Place the fillets in a 13-in. x 9-in. baking dish coated with cooking spray. In a small bowl, combine the soup, lemon juice and sherry or broth. Pour over fillets. Bake, uncovered, at 350° for 20 minutes.

2 In a small nonstick skillet, saute onion in butter for 2 minutes. Add garlic; cook 1 minute longer. Stir in bread crumbs and Worcestershire sauce. Sprinkle over fillets. Bake 5-10 minutes longer or until fish flakes easily with a fork.

YIELD: 6 SERVINGS.

Here's a main course that's impressive enough for guests but simple enough for weeknights. The moist stuffing only takes a few moments to prepare.

Kimberly Andresen
Chiefland, FL

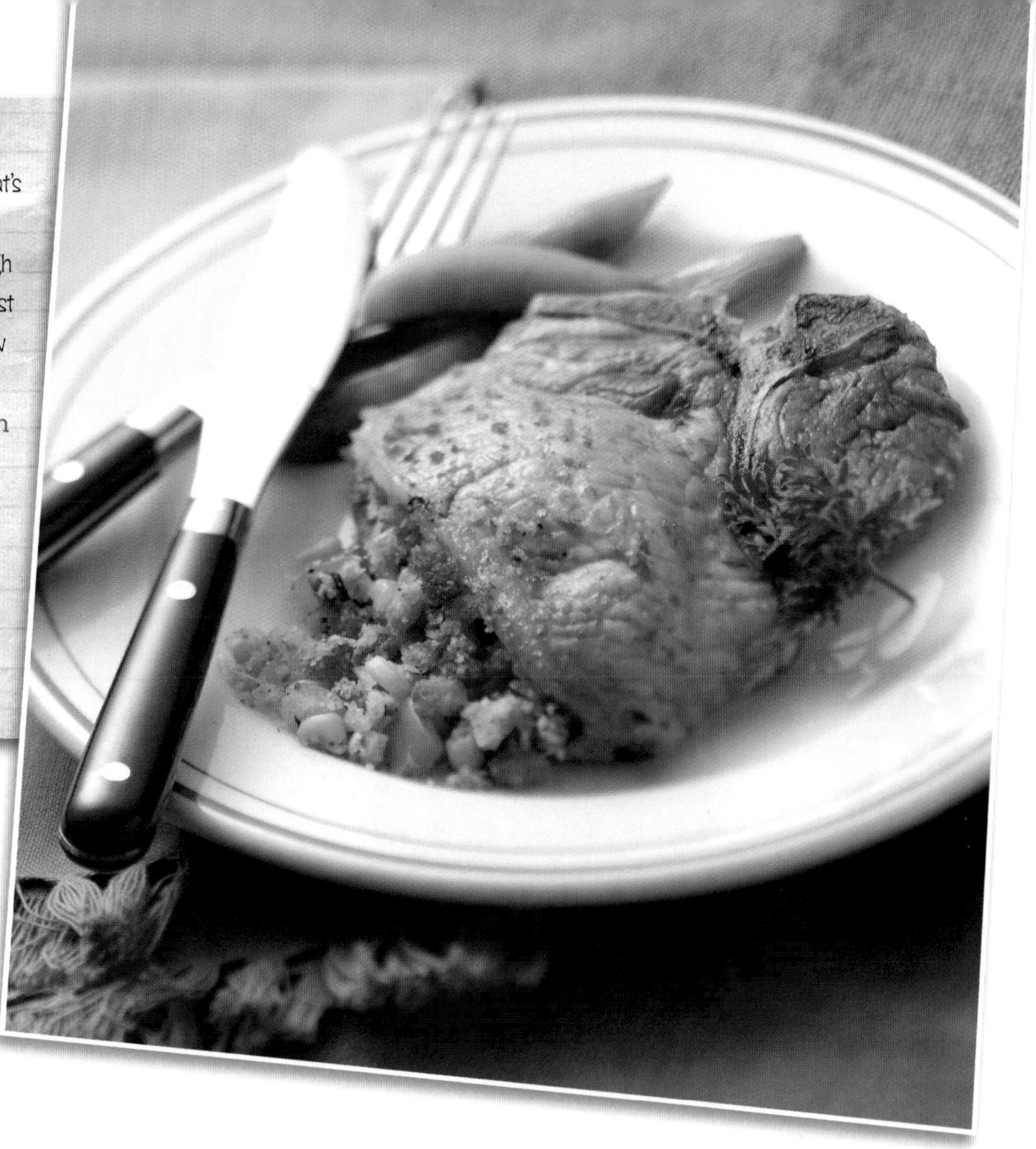

corn-stuffed pork chops

PREP: 15 MIN. BAKE: 35 MIN.

- 1/4 cup chopped onion
- 1/4 cup chopped green pepper
- 1 tablespoon butter
- 3/4 cup corn bread stuffing mix
- 1/2 cup frozen corn, thawed
- 2 tablespoons diced pimientos
- 1/4 teaspoon salt
- 1/8 teaspoon ground cumin
- 1/8 teaspoon pepper
- 4 bone-in pork loin chops (7 ounces each)

1 In a large skillet, saute the onion and green pepper in butter for 3-4 minutes or until tender. Stir in the corn bread stuffing mix, corn, pimientos, salt, cumin and pepper.

2 Cut a pocket in each chop by slicing almost to the bone. Stuff each chop with the mixture. Secure with toothpicks if necessary.

3 Place in an 11-in. x 7-in. baking dish that is coated with cooking spray. Bake, uncovered, at 375° for 35-40 minutes or until a meat thermometer inserted into the thickest portion of the meat reads 160°. Discard toothpicks.

YIELD: 4 SERVINGS.

turkey wafflewiches

PREP/TOTAL TIME: 15 MIN.

1 package (3 ounces) cream cheese, softened
1/4 cup whole-berry cranberry sauce
1 tablespoon maple pancake syrup
1/4 teaspoon pepper
8 slices white bread
3/4 pound sliced deli turkey
2 tablespoons butter, softened

1 In a small bowl, beat the cream cheese, cranberry sauce, syrup and pepper until combined. Spread over four slices of bread; top with turkey and remaining bread. Spread butter over both sides of sandwiches.

2 Cook in a preheated waffle iron or on an indoor grill according to the manufacturer's directions for 2-3 minutes or until golden brown.

YIELD: 4 SERVINGS.

Who knew sandwiches could be so fun? This unique combination brings smiles to the whole table with its fantastic flavor and whimsical appearance.
Taste of Home Test Kitchen

italian turkey sandwich loaf

PREP: 15 MIN. BAKE: 40 MIN. + STANDING

One wedge of this sandwich goes a long way. Each bite is packed with turkey, cheese and vegetables.

Joan Camello • Holmdel, NJ

1 round loaf (1 pound) Italian bread
1/4 cup Italian salad dressing
12 fresh baby spinach leaves
1 cup (4 ounces) shredded part-skim mozzarella cheese
1/2 pound thinly sliced deli turkey
3/4 cup thinly sliced peeled cucumber
1 medium tomato, sliced

1 Cut a 1-in. slice off top of bread and set aside. Carefully hollow out loaf, leaving a 1/2-in. shell (save removed bread for another use). Brush inside of bread with salad dressing.

2 In the bread shell, layer the spinach, 1/2 cup mozzarella cheese, turkey, cucumber, tomato and remaining cheese. Replace the bread top; wrap loaf in foil.

3 Place on a baking sheet. Bake at 350° for 40-45 minutes or until heated through. Let stand for 10 minutes before cutting into wedges.

YIELD: 6 SERVINGS.

Canned soup makes this elegant classic so quick and easy, while pimientos, celery and green pepper add both color and crunch. It's a great recipe for using up leftover chicken.

Jennifer Eggebraate
Delton, MI

chicken a la king

PREP/TOTAL TIME: 20 MIN.

1/2 cup chopped celery

1/2 cup chopped green pepper

2 tablespoons butter

2 cans (10-3/4 ounces each) condensed cream of chicken soup, undiluted

1 cup whole milk

1/4 teaspoon pepper

2 cups cubed cooked chicken

1 jar (6 ounces) sliced mushrooms, drained

1/4 cup diced pimientos

6 slices bread, toasted and halved

1 In a large skillet, saute celery and green pepper in butter until crisp-tender. Stir in the soup, milk and pepper. Add the chicken, mushrooms and pimientos. Reduce heat; simmer, uncovered, for 4-6 minutes or until heated through. Serve over toast.

YIELD: 4 SERVINGS.

beef-stuffed french bread

PREP: 25 MIN. BAKE: 20 MIN. + CHILLING

1 pound ground beef

1/2 cup chopped onion

1 large baked potato, peeled and cubed

1 can (10-3/4 ounces) condensed cream of mushroom soup, undiluted

1 can (4 ounces) mushroom stems and pieces, drained

1 teaspoon dried parsley flakes

1/4 teaspoon garlic powder

1/8 teaspoon pepper

Dash hot pepper sauce

1 loaf (1 pound) French bread

1 cup (4 ounces) shredded cheddar cheese

1 In a large skillet, cook the beef and onion over medium heat until meat is no longer pink; drain. Add the potato, soup, mushrooms, parsley, garlic powder, pepper and hot pepper sauce; cover and simmer for 10 minutes.

2 Meanwhile, cut the loaf of bread in half lengthwise. Hollow out bottom of loaf, leaving a 3/4-in. shell; set aside. Place the removed bread in a blender; cover and process until crumbled. Add 1 cup of crumbs to beef mixture (save remaining crumbs for another use). Stir in cheese.

3 Spoon beef mixture into bread shell; replace bread top. Wrap in heavy-duty foil; place on a baking sheet. Bake at 350° for 20 minutes. Let stand for 5 minutes before slicing.

YIELD: 6-8 SERVINGS.

Flour tortillas are available in a variety of flavors, including sun-dried tomato, spinach and whole wheat. Serve chips with the extra guacamole to accompany the sandwiches.

Taste of Home Test Kitchen

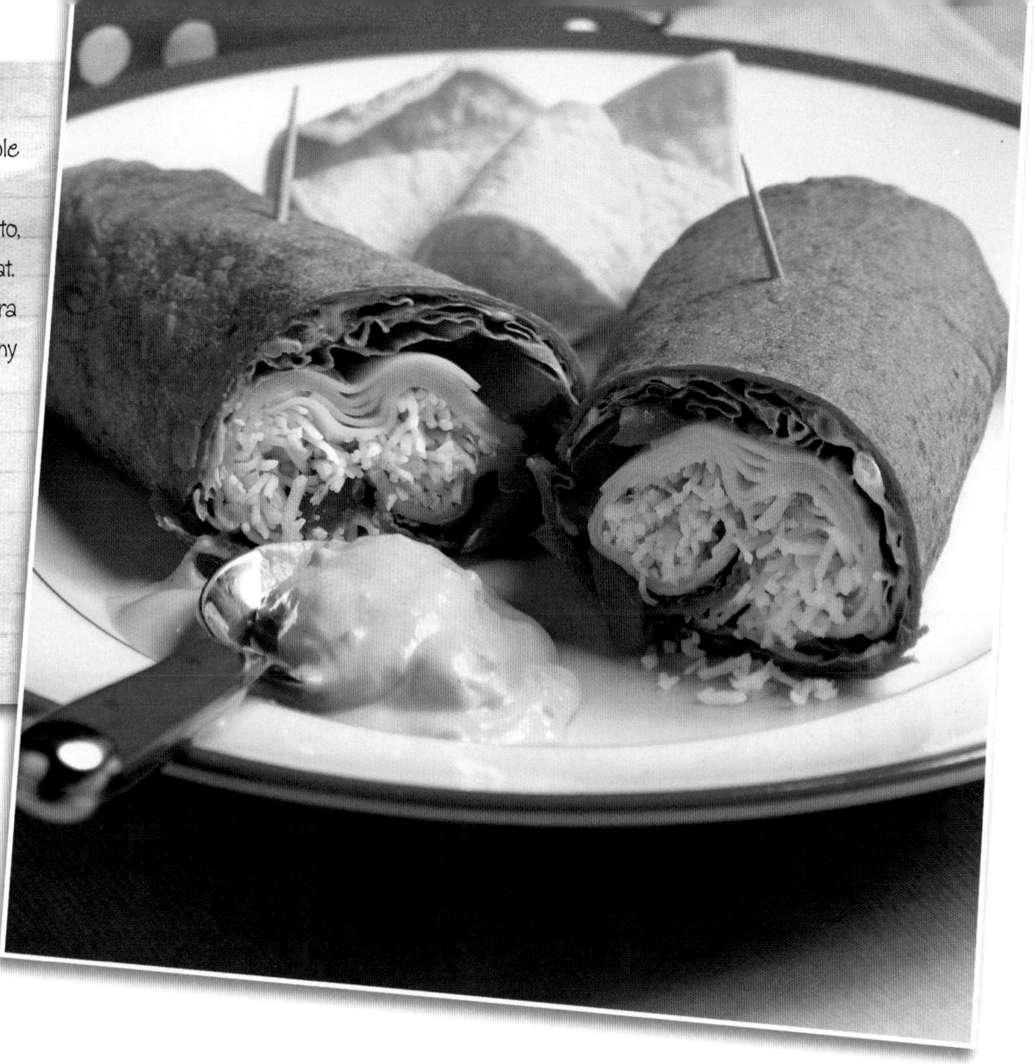

guacamole chicken roll-ups

PREP/TOTAL TIME: 15 MIN.

- 1/4 cup guacamole
- 4 flavored flour tortillas of your choice (10 inches)
- 4 large lettuce leaves
- 1-1/3 cups chopped fresh tomatoes
- 2 packages (6 ounces each) thinly sliced deli smoked chicken breast
- 2 cups (8 ounces) shredded Mexican cheese blend

1 Spread 1 tablespoon of guacamole over each tortilla. Layer with lettuce, tomatoes, chicken and cheese. Roll up tightly.

YIELD: 4 SERVINGS.

extra tortillas

For a quick quesadilla, spread shredded cheese and salsa on a tortilla and top with another tortilla. Pop it in the oven and bake until cheese melts. Cut into wedges and serve warm.

beef sirloin tip roast

PREP: 10 MIN. BAKE: 2-1/2 HOURS

- 1 beef sirloin tip roast (3 pounds)
- 1-1/4 cups water, divided
- 1 can (8 ounces) mushroom stems and pieces, drained
- 1 envelope onion soup mix
- 2 tablespoons cornstarch

1 Place a large piece of heavy-duty foil (21 in. x 17 in.) in a shallow roasting pan. Place roast on foil. Pour 1 cup water and mushrooms over roast. Sprinkle with soup mix. Wrap foil around the roast and seal tightly.

2 Bake at 350° for 2-1/2 to 3 hours or until the meat reaches the desired doneness (for medium-rare, a meat thermometer should read 145°; medium, 160°; well-done, 170°). Remove the roast to a serving platter and keep warm.

3 Pour the drippings and mushrooms into a saucepan. Combine the cornstarch and remaining water until smooth; gradually stir into the drippings. Bring to a boil; cook and stir for 2 minutes or until thickened. Serve with sliced beef.

YIELD: 10-12 SERVINGS.

making a sauce

To use cornstarch to thicken sauce, dissolve the cornstarch in a small amount of a cold liquid before slowly adding it to a hot mixture. Then, to make a nicely thickened sauce, cook and stir the mixture for a full 2 minutes.

pineapple shrimp kabobs

PREP: 30 MIN. + MARINATING GRILL: 10 MIN.

2 cans (20 ounces each) pineapple chunks

2 cups fat-free Italian salad dressing

2 cans (8 ounces each) tomato sauce

1/4 cup packed brown sugar

2 teaspoons prepared mustard

2 pounds uncooked medium shrimp, peeled and deveined (about 64)

4 large sweet red peppers, cut into chunks

2 large onions, cut into chunks

1 Drain pineapple, reserving 1/2 cup juice; refrigerate pineapple. In a small bowl, combine the salad dressing, tomato sauce, brown sugar, mustard and reserved juice. Pour 3 cups into a large resealable plastic bag; add the shrimp. Seal bag and turn to coat; refrigerate for 3 hours. Cover and refrigerate remaining marinade for basting.

2 Drain and discard marinade from shrimp. On 16 metal or soaked wooden skewers, alternately thread the shrimp, red peppers, onions and pineapple. Using long-handled tongs, dip a paper towel in cooking oil and lightly coat the grill rack.

3 Grill, covered, over medium heat or broil 4 in. from the heat for 6-10 minutes or until shrimp turn pink and vegetables are tender, turning and basting occasionally with reserved marinade.

YIELD: 8 SERVINGS.

chicken wraps

PREP/TOTAL TIME: 25 MIN.

16 frozen breaded chicken tenders

1/2 cup ranch salad dressing

4 sun-dried tomato tortillas (10 inches),
   room temperature

3 cups shredded lettuce

1 can (2-1/4 ounces) sliced ripe olives, drained

4 slices pepper Jack cheese

Hot pepper sauce, optional

1 Bake chicken according to package directions. Meanwhile, spread 2 tablespoons salad dressing over each tortilla. Sprinkle lettuce and olives down the center of each tortilla. Top with cheese and chicken; drizzle with hot pepper sauce if desired. Roll up; secure with toothpicks.

YIELD: 4 SERVINGS.

dressed-up steaks

PREP/TOTAL TIME: 20 MIN.

1 tablespoon olive oil

1-1/2 teaspoons minced garlic

1 teaspoon dried oregano

1 teaspoon pepper

4 beef top sirloin steaks (6 ounces each)

3/4 cup Catalina salad dressing, divided

1 In a small bowl, combine the oil, garlic, oregano and pepper. Rub over both sides of steaks. Brush with 1/4 cup salad dressing. Place on a broiler pan.

2 Broil 4 in. from the heat for 5-6 minutes on each side or until meat reaches desired doneness (for medium-rare, a meat thermometer should read 145°; medium, 160°; well-done, 170°). Serve with remaining dressing.

YIELD: 4 SERVINGS.

Just five pantry ingredients nicely season these special-looking broiled steaks that are accented with extra salad dressing.

Taste of Home Test Kitchen

bacon chicken skewers

PREP: 15 MIN. + MARINATING GRILL: 10 MIN.

Your whole family will fall for these moist, flavorful chicken strips. I serve them every year at my daughter's birthday party because her friends request them!

Lynn Lackner • Worth, IL

1/2 cup ranch salad dressing

1/2 cup barbecue sauce

1 teaspoon chili powder

2 drops hot pepper sauce

1-1/4 pounds boneless skinless chicken breasts, cut into 12 strips

12 bacon strips

1 In a large resealable plastic bag, combine the ranch dressing, barbecue sauce, chili powder and hot pepper sauce; add chicken. Seal bag and turn to coat; refrigerate for at least 2 hours.

2 In a large skillet, cook the bacon strips over medium heat until partially cooked but not crisp. Drain on paper towels.

3 Drain and discard marinade. Place a chicken strip on each bacon strip; thread each onto a metal or soaked wooden skewer.

4 Grill skewers, covered, over medium heat or broil 4-6 in. from the heat for 10-14 minutes or until juices run clear, turning occasionally.

YIELD: 6 SERVINGS.

meat loaf wellington

PREP: 20 MIN. BAKE: 1-1/4 HOURS

1 egg, lightly beaten

1 cup meatless spaghetti sauce, divided

1/4 cup dry bread crumbs

1/2 teaspoon salt

1/4 teaspoon pepper

1-1/2 pounds ground beef

2 cups (8 ounces) shredded part-skim mozzarella cheese, divided

1 tablespoon minced fresh parsley

1 tube (8 ounces) refrigerated crescent rolls

1 In a large bowl, combine the egg, 1/3 cup spaghetti sauce, bread crumbs, salt and pepper. Crumble beef over mixture and mix well.

2 On a piece of heavy-duty foil, pat beef mixture into a 12-in. x 8-in. rectangle. Sprinkle 1 cup cheese and parsley to within 1 in. of edges. Roll up jelly-roll style, starting with a long side and peeling foil away while rolling. Seal seam and ends. Place seam side down in a greased 13-in. x 9-in. baking dish.

3 Bake, uncovered, at 350° for 1 hour; drain. Unroll crescent dough; seal seams and perforations. Drape dough over meat loaf to cover the top, sides and ends; seal ends. Bake 15-20 minutes longer or until a meat thermometer reads 160° and crust is golden brown. Let stand for 5 minutes.

4 Meanwhile, warm remaining spaghetti sauce. Using two large spatulas, carefully transfer meat loaf to a serving platter. Sprinkle with remaining cheese. Serve with spaghetti sauce.

YIELD: 8 SERVINGS.

guacamole turkey blts

PREP/TOTAL TIME: 15 MIN.

12 slices ready-to-serve fully cooked bacon

3/4 cup guacamole

12 slices whole wheat bread, toasted

6 large lettuce leaves

12 slices tomato

1 pound thinly sliced deli turkey

1 Heat bacon according to package directions. Spread 1 tablespoon of guacamole over six pieces of toast. Layer with lettuce, tomato, bacon and turkey. Spread remaining guacamole over remaining toast; place over turkey.

YIELD: 6 SERVINGS.

Want to jazz up your turkey sandwiches? Grab some guacamole from the produce department.

Taste of Home Test Kitchen

spinach-stuffed salmon

PREP/TOTAL TIME: 30 MIN.

These moist salmon fillets are filled with spinach, pesto, sun-dried tomatoes and pine nuts. They're pretty and delicious!

Betty Stewart • Leola, PA

2 thick-cut salmon fillets (5 ounces each)

Dash salt and pepper

2 cups packed fresh baby spinach

1 tablespoon prepared pesto

1 tablespoon sun-dried tomatoes (not packed in oil), chopped

1 tablespoon pine nuts

1 Cut a horizontal pocket in each salmon fillet by slicing to within 1/2 in. of opposite side. Sprinkle with salt and pepper. In a small bowl, combine the spinach, pesto, tomatoes and pine nuts. Spoon into each pocket.

2 Place salmon on a broiler pan coated with cooking spray. Broil 4-6 in. from the heat for 12-15 minutes or until spinach mixture is heated through and fish flakes easily with a fork.

YIELD: 2 SERVINGS.

finished fish

For fish fillets, check for doneness by inserting a fork at an angle into the thickest portion of the fish and gently parting the meat. When it is opaque and flakes into sections, it is cooked completely.

chicken 'n' broccoli braid

PREP: 25 MIN. BAKE: 15 MIN.

Beautiful braided breads really dress up events. My buttery loaf is stuffed with chicken and veggies. I love to make this simple, tasty dish for my family.

Dana Rabe • West Richland, WA

- 2 cups cubed cooked chicken
- 1 cup chopped fresh broccoli
- 1 cup (4 ounces) shredded sharp cheddar cheese
- 1/2 cup chopped sweet red pepper
- 2 teaspoons dill weed
- 1 garlic clove, minced
- 1/4 teaspoon salt
- 1/2 cup mayonnaise
- 2 tubes (8 ounces each) refrigerated crescent rolls
- 1 egg white, lightly beaten
- 2 tablespoons slivered almonds

1 In a large bowl, combine the first seven ingredients. Stir in mayonnaise. Unroll both tubes of crescent dough onto an ungreased baking sheet; press together, forming a 15-in. x 12-in. rectangle. Seal seams and perforations. Spoon filling lengthwise down the center third of dough.

2 On each long side, cut dough 3 in. toward the center at 1-1/2-in. intervals, forming strips. Bring one strip from each side over filling; pinch ends to seal. Repeat. Pinch ends of loaf to seal.

3 Brush with egg white; sprinkle with almonds. Bake at 375° for 15-20 minutes or until crust is golden brown and filling is heated through.

YIELD: 8 SERVINGS.

You can use your favorite brand of frozen breaded fish in this recipe.
Taste of Home Test Kitchen

fish po'boys

PREP/TOTAL TIME: 30 MIN.

- 2 packages (11.4 ounces each) frozen crunchy breaded fish fillets
- 1/2 cup mayonnaise
- 1 tablespoon minced fresh parsley
- 1 tablespoon ketchup
- 2 teaspoons stone-ground mustard
- 1 teaspoon horseradish sauce
- 2 to 4 drops hot pepper sauce
- 1-1/2 cups deli coleslaw
- 6 hamburger buns, split

1 Bake fish according to the package directions. Meanwhile, in a small bowl, combine the mayonnaise, parsley, ketchup, mustard, horseradish sauce and hot pepper sauce until blended. Spoon 1/4 cup coleslaw onto the bottom of each bun; top with two pieces of fish. Spread with sauce; replace bun tops.

YIELD: 6 SERVINGS.

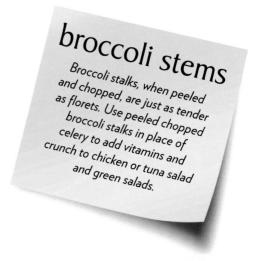

broccoli stems

Broccoli stalks, when peeled and chopped, are just as tender as florets. Use peeled chopped broccoli stalks in place of celery to add vitamins and crunch to chicken or tuna salad and green salads.

bacon avocado wraps

PREP/TOTAL TIME: 15 MIN.

1/3 cup mayonnaise

2 tablespoons chipotle sauce

1 tablespoon sour cream

1 package (2.1 ounces) ready-to-serve fully cooked bacon

4 flour tortillas (8 inches)

4 large lettuce leaves

1 large tomato, sliced

2 medium ripe avocados, peeled and sliced

1 In a small bowl, combine the mayonnaise, chipotle sauce and sour cream until smooth. Heat bacon according to package directions. Spread chipotle mayonnaise over tortillas; layer with lettuce, tomato, bacon and avocados. Roll up tightly.

YIELD: 4 SERVINGS.

Using one recipe to serve a whole meal is a dream come true for busy cooks. These delicious dinners are quick, easy and family friendly.

all-in-one dinners

weekday lasagna

PREP: 35 MIN. BAKE: 1 HOUR + STANDING

1 pound lean ground beef (90% lean)

1 small onion, chopped

1 can (28 ounces) crushed tomatoes

1-3/4 cups water

1 can (6 ounces) tomato paste

1 envelope spaghetti sauce mix

1 egg, lightly beaten

2 cups (16 ounces) fat-free cottage cheese

2 tablespoons grated Parmesan cheese

6 uncooked lasagna noodles

1 cup (4 ounces) shredded part-skim mozzarella cheese

1 In a large saucepan, cook beef and onion over medium heat until meat is no longer pink; drain. Stir in the tomatoes, water, tomato paste and spaghetti sauce mix. Bring to a boil. Reduce heat; cover and simmer for 15-20 minutes, stirring occasionally.

2 In a small bowl, combine the egg, cottage cheese and Parmesan cheese. Spread 2 cups meat sauce in a 13-in. x 9-in. baking dish coated with cooking spray. Layer with three noodles, half of cottage cheese mixture and half of remaining meat sauce. Repeat layers.

3 Cover and bake at 350° for 50 minutes or until a thermometer reads 160°. Uncover; sprinkle with mozzarella cheese. Bake 10-15 minutes longer or until bubbly and cheese is melted. Let stand for 15 minutes before cutting.

YIELD: 9 SERVINGS.

chicken broccoli calzones

PREP: 20 MIN. BAKE: 20 MIN.

3 cups frozen chopped broccoli
1/2 teaspoon rubbed sage
1 small onion, finely chopped
3 garlic cloves, minced
1 tablespoon olive oil
2 cups shredded cooked chicken breast
1/2 pound smoked mozzarella cheese, shredded
1/3 cup chopped fresh basil
1/3 cup golden raisins
1 loaf (1 pound) frozen bread dough, thawed
1 egg
1 tablespoon water

1 Cook broccoli according to package directions; drain. Sprinkle with sage; set aside. In a large saucepan, saute onion and garlic in oil until tender. Remove from the heat. Stir in the broccoli, chicken, cheese, basil and raisins; set aside.

2 On a lightly floured surface, divide dough into four pieces. Roll each piece into a 10-in. circle. Carefully place one circle on a lightly greased baking sheet. Spoon a fourth of the chicken mixture onto half of the circle. Brush edges of dough with water; fold dough over filling and pinch edges to seal. Repeat with remaining dough and filling.

3 With a sharp knife, make two slashes on each calzone. Beat the egg and water; brush over the calzones. Bake at 400° for 18-22 minutes or until golden brown.

YIELD: 4 CALZONES.

mexican pizza

PREP/TOTAL TIME: 30 MIN.

1 large onion

1 prebaked 12-inch pizza crust

1 can (16 ounces) refried beans

2 cups (8 ounces) shredded cheddar cheese

3 cups shredded lettuce

1 cup (4 ounces) shredded Mexican cheese blend

1/3 cup chopped seeded tomato

2 tablespoons sliced ripe olives

1/2 cup coarsely chopped ranch-flavored tortilla chips

1 Slice half of the onion and chop the rest; set aside. Place crust on an ungreased 12-in. pizza pan. Spread beans over crust to within 1/2 in. of edges. Top with cheddar cheese and sliced onion.

2 Bake at 450° for 10-12 minutes or until cheese is melted. Top with lettuce, Mexican cheese, chopped onion, tomato, olives and tortilla chips.

YIELD: 8 SLICES.

no more seeds
To remove the seeds from a tomato, cut it in half horizontally and remove the stem. Holding a tomato half over a bowl or sink, scrape out seeds with a small spoon or squeeze the tomato to force out the seeds.

Speed up the prep time for this easy recipe by purchasing a tin of ready-to-eat corn bread from the bakery section of your local grocery store.

Taste of Home Test Kitchen

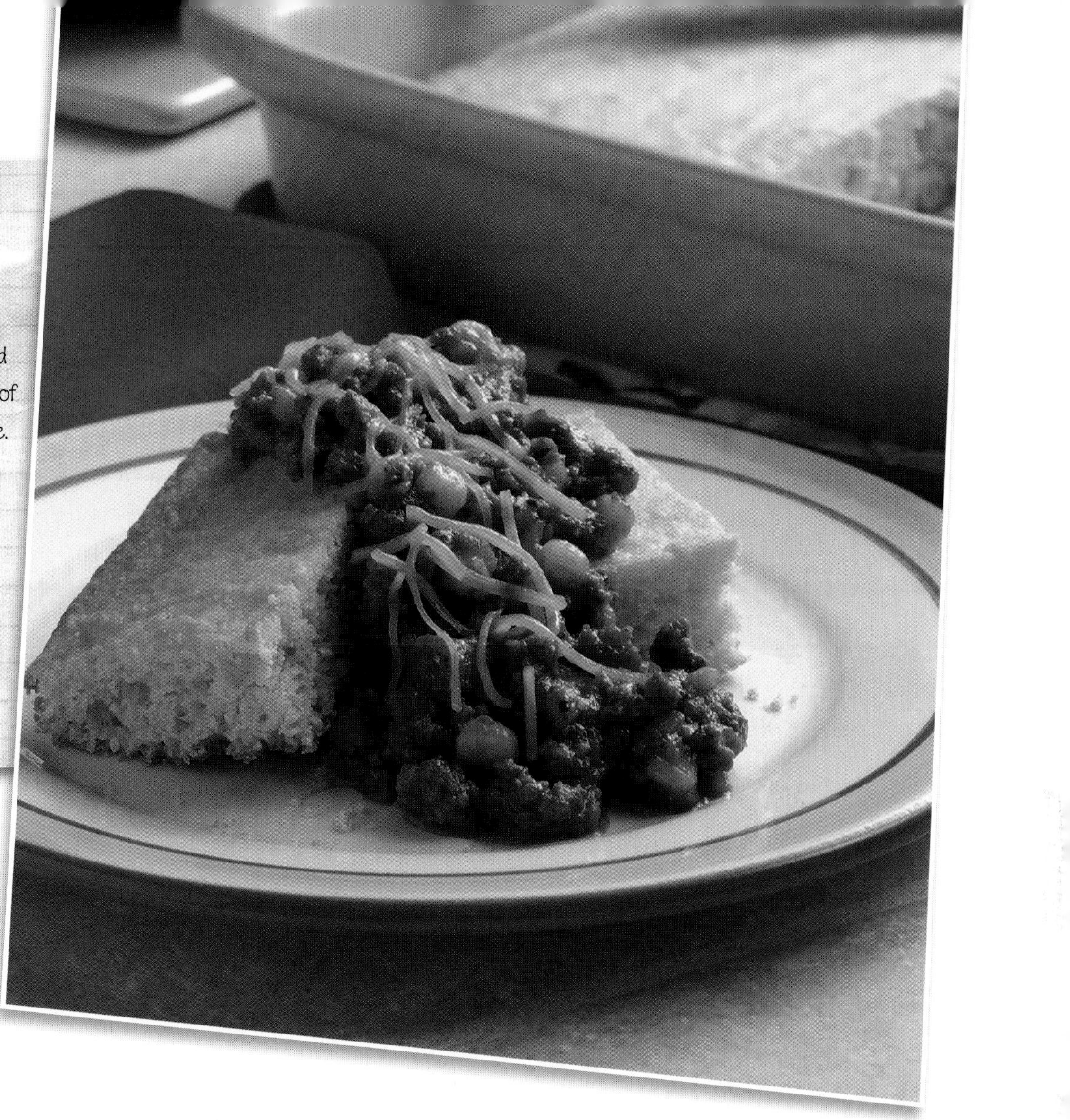

corn bread sloppy joes

PREP/TOTAL TIME: 30 MIN.

1 package (8-1/2 ounces) corn bread/muffin mix
1 egg
1/3 cup whole milk
2 pounds ground beef
1/2 cup chopped onion
1 jar (26 ounces) meatless spaghetti sauce
1 cup frozen corn
1 can (4 ounces) chopped green chilies, drained
2 envelopes sloppy joe mix
1 cup (4 ounces) shredded cheddar cheese

1 Prepare and bake corn bread according to package directions, using the egg and milk. Meanwhile, in a large skillet, cook beef and onion over medium heat until meat is no longer pink; drain. Stir in the spaghetti sauce, corn, chilies and sloppy joe mix. Bring to a boil. Reduce heat; simmer, uncovered, for 10 minutes.

2 Sprinkle with cheese; cover and cook for 1 minute or until cheese is melted. Cut corn bread into six pieces; cut each piece in half. Top with the sloppy joe mixture.

YIELD: 6 SERVINGS.

biscuit mushroom bake

PREP: 20 MIN. BAKE: 15 MIN.

1 pound sliced fresh mushrooms

2 tablespoons butter

3 tablespoons all-purpose flour

1 cup chicken broth

1/2 cup whole milk

1 tablespoon lemon juice

1 teaspoon onion powder

1 teaspoon garlic powder

1/4 teaspoon salt

1/4 teaspoon pepper

1/4 teaspoon paprika

1 tube (12 ounces) refrigerated biscuits

1 In a large skillet, saute mushrooms in butter. Stir in flour until blended. Gradually add broth and milk. Bring to a boil; cook and stir for 2 minutes or until thickened. Remove from the heat. Stir in the lemon juice, onion powder, garlic powder, salt, pepper and paprika.

2 Pour into a greased 11-in. x 7-in. baking dish. Arrange biscuits over the top. Bake, uncovered, at 375° for 15-20 minutes or until biscuits are golden brown. Let stand for 5 minutes before serving.

YIELD: 5 SERVINGS.

spaghetti casserole

PREP: 15 MIN. BAKE: 25 MIN.

This quick hot dish makes great use of convenience products like canned spaghetti sauce and jarred mushrooms, and children will love how cheesy it is.

Pat Richter • Lake Placid, FL

- 1-1/2 pounds ground beef
- 1 cup chopped green pepper
- 1/2 cup chopped onion
- 1 teaspoon salt
- 1/2 teaspoon pepper
- 1 teaspoon minced garlic
- 3 cans (14-3/4 ounces each) spaghetti in tomato sauce with cheese
- 1 jar (6 ounces) sliced mushrooms, drained
- 1 can (2-1/4 ounces) sliced ripe olives, drained
- 2 cups (8 ounces) shredded cheddar cheese
- 1 cup grated Parmesan cheese

1 In a large skillet, cook the beef, green pepper, onion, salt and pepper over medium-high heat for 10-12 minutes or until meat is no longer pink. Add garlic; cook 1 minute longer. Drain. Stir in the spaghetti, mushrooms and olives.

2 Transfer to two greased 8-in. square baking dishes. Sprinkle with cheeses. Cover and freeze one casserole for up to 3 months. Bake remaining casserole, uncovered, at 350° for 25-30 minutes or until bubbly and golden brown.

3 **To use frozen casserole:** Remove from the freezer 30 minutes before baking (do not thaw). Cover and bake at 350° for 1 hour. Uncover; bake 15-20 minutes longer or until heated through.

YIELD: 2 CASSEROLES (4 SERVINGS EACH).

My family, kids and adults alike, loves this quick take on an all-time classic!
Krendi Ford • Belleville, MI

ravioli with sausage

PREP/TOTAL TIME: 20 MIN.

- 4 cups frozen cheese ravioli (about 12 ounces)
- 1/2 pound smoked sausage, sliced
- 1 cup chopped green pepper
- 1 jar (26 ounces) meatless spaghetti sauce
- 1/4 cup shredded Parmesan cheese

1 Cook ravioli according to package directions. Meanwhile, in a large skillet, saute sausage and green pepper for 2-3 minutes or until green pepper is tender. Stir in spaghetti sauce; heat through. Drain ravioli; toss with sausage mixture. Sprinkle with cheese.

YIELD: 5 SERVINGS.

italian sausage with polenta

PREP: 15 MIN. COOK: 25 MIN.

1 package (19-1/2 ounces) Italian turkey sausage links, casings removed

1/2 cup chopped red onion

4 garlic cloves, minced

2-1/2 cups fresh broccoli florets

2 cans (15 ounces each) crushed tomatoes

2 tablespoons prepared pesto

1/2 teaspoon crushed red pepper flakes

1/4 teaspoon pepper

3 cups reduced-sodium chicken broth

1 cup cornmeal

Shaved Parmesan cheese, optional

1 In a large nonstick skillet coated with cooking spray, cook sausage and onion over medium heat until meat is no longer pink. Add garlic; cook 1 minute longer. Stir in broccoli. Reduce heat; cover and cook for 5-7 minutes or until broccoli is tender.

2 Stir in the tomatoes, pesto, pepper flakes and pepper; bring to a boil. Reduce heat; simmer, uncovered, for 10 minutes.

3 Meanwhile, for polenta, bring broth to a boil in a small heavy saucepan. Reduce heat to a gentle boil; slowly whisk in cornmeal. Continue stirring for 10-12 minutes or until polenta is thickened and has a smooth texture. Serve with sausage mixture. Garnish with cheese if desired.

YIELD: 6 SERVINGS.

This crunchy, saucy hot dish is potluck-perfect! It's so convenient because you can make the casserole the day before and bake it the day of the party. It's good made with turkey, too.

Joyce Wilson
Omaha, NE

make-ahead chicken bake

PREP: 25 MIN. + CHILLING BAKE: 30 MIN.

5 cups cubed cooked chicken

2 cups chopped celery

5 hard-cooked eggs, sliced

1 can (10-3/4 ounces) condensed cream of chicken soup, undiluted

3/4 cup mayonnaise

2 tablespoons lemon juice

1 tablespoon pimientos, optional

1 teaspoon finely chopped onion

1 cup (4 ounces) shredded cheddar cheese

1 can (3 ounces) chow mein noodles

1/2 cup slivered almonds, toasted

1 In a large bowl, combine the first eight ingredients. Transfer to a greased 3-qt. baking dish; sprinkle with cheese, chow mein noodles and almonds. Cover and refrigerate overnight.

2 Remove from the refrigerator 30 minutes before baking. Bake, uncovered, at 350° for 30-35 minutes until lightly browned and cheese is bubbly.

YIELD: 12 SERVINGS.

apricot beef stir-fry

PREP/TOTAL TIME: 25 MIN.

1 teaspoon cornstarch

1/4 cup cold water

1/2 cup apricot preserves

2 tablespoons soy sauce

1/2 teaspoon minced garlic

1/4 teaspoon salt

1/4 teaspoon crushed red pepper flakes

1 pound beef top sirloin steak, thinly sliced

1 tablespoon canola oil

1 package (16 ounces) frozen asparagus stir-fry vegetable blend

Hot cooked rice

1 In a small bowl, whisk cornstarch and cold water until smooth. Stir in the apricot preserves, soy sauce, garlic, salt and pepper flakes; set aside.

2 In a large skillet or wok, stir-fry beef in oil until no longer pink; remove and keep warm. In the same pan, stir-fry vegetable blend according to package directions. Return beef to the pan. Stir apricot mixture and add to beef mixture. Cook and stir until slightly thickened. Serve with rice.

YIELD: 4 SERVINGS.

jalapeno chicken pizza

PREP/TOTAL TIME: 25 MIN.

2 plum tomatoes, quartered

1/2 cup fresh cilantro leaves

1 tablespoon tomato paste

1 teaspoon chopped chipotle peppers in adobo sauce

1 garlic clove, peeled and quartered

1/2 teaspoon salt

1 prebaked 12-inch thin pizza crust

2 cups shredded cooked chicken breast

3/4 cup shredded reduced-fat Monterey Jack cheese or Mexican cheese blend

2 jalapeno peppers, seeded and sliced into rings

1 Place the first six ingredients in a food processor; cover and process until blended. Place the crust on an ungreased 12-in. pizza pan; spread with tomato mixture. Top with chicken, cheese and jalapenos.

2 Bake at 450° for 10-12 minutes or until heated through and cheese is melted.

YIELD: 12 PIECES.

EDITOR'S NOTE: When cutting hot peppers, disposable gloves are recommended. Avoid touching your face.

Chipotle is a...

...smoked, dried jalapeno pepper originating near Mexico City and often found canned in a chili sauce in the United States. Chipotles are medium to hot in heat levels and are used in a variety of spicy dishes.

This pasta is filling and tastes great! The pesto flavor makes a meal your gang will love.

Taste of Home Test Kitchen

spinach tuna casserole

PREP: 25 MIN. BAKE: 50 MIN.

This thick, gooey casserole has been a family favorite for years.

Karla Hamrick • Wapakoneta, OH

- 5 cups uncooked egg noodles
- 2 cups (16 ounces) sour cream
- 1-1/2 cups mayonnaise
- 2 to 3 teaspoons lemon juice
- 2 to 3 teaspoons whole milk
- 1/4 teaspoon salt
- 1 package (10 ounces) frozen chopped spinach, thawed and squeezed dry
- 1 package (6 ounces) chicken stuffing mix
- 1/3 cup seasoned bread crumbs
- 1 can (6 ounces) tuna, drained and flaked
- 3 tablespoons grated Parmesan cheese

1 Cook noodles according to package directions. Meanwhile, in a large bowl, combine the sour cream, mayonnaise, lemon juice, milk and salt. Stir in the spinach, stuffing mix, bread crumbs and tuna until well combined.

2 Drain noodles and place in a greased 13-in. x 9-in. baking dish. Top with tuna mixture; sprinkle with cheese. Cover and bake at 350° for 45 minutes. Uncover; bake 5-10 minutes longer or until lightly browned and heated through.

YIELD: 8 SERVINGS.

pesto chicken pasta

PREP/TOTAL TIME: 20 MIN.

- 1 package (16 ounces) cellentani or spiral pasta
- 2 cups cubed rotisserie chicken
- 1 cup chopped fresh tomatoes
- 1 container (7 ounces) prepared pesto
- 1/4 cup pine nuts, toasted

1 Cook pasta according to package directions. Meanwhile, in a nonstick skillet, saute chicken and tomatoes for 2 minutes. Stir in pesto; heat through. Drain pasta; toss with chicken mixture. Sprinkle with pine nuts.

YIELD: 6 SERVINGS.

more on pasta

Cooking times vary with the size and variety of pasta. Dried pasta can take from 5 to 15 minutes to cook; fresh pasta can cook in as little as 2 to 3 minutes. Follow the recommended cooking directions on packaged pasta.

lattice chicken potpie

PREP: 10 MIN. BAKE: 35 MIN.

1 package (16 ounces) frozen California-blend vegetables

2 cups cubed cooked chicken

1 can (10-3/4 ounces) condensed cream of potato soup, undiluted

1 cup whole milk

1 cup (4 ounces) shredded cheddar cheese

1 can (2.8 ounces) french-fried onions

1/2 teaspoon seasoned salt

1 tube (8 ounces) refrigerated crescent rolls

1 In a large bowl, combine the vegetables, chicken, soup, milk, cheese, onions and seasoned salt. Transfer to a greased shallow 2-qt. baking dish.

2 Unroll the crescent roll dough and separate into two rectangles. Seal the perforations; cut each rectangle lengthwise into 1/2-in. strips. Form a lattice crust over the chicken mixture. Bake, uncovered, at 375° for 35-40 minutes or until golden brown.

YIELD: 4-6 SERVINGS.

asian pork
tenderloin salad

PREP: 10 MIN. + MARINATING COOK: 5 MIN.

1 can (15 ounces) apricot halves
1/4 cup soy sauce
1 tablespoon brown sugar
1 tablespoon canola oil
1/2 teaspoon ground ginger
1/2 teaspoon minced garlic
1/4 teaspoon ground mustard
1 pork tenderloin (1 pound), thinly sliced
2 packages (9-3/4 ounces each)
   Asian crunch salad mix

1 Drain apricots, reserving 1/2 cup juice; set apricots aside. In a large resealable plastic bag, combine the soy sauce, brown sugar, oil, ginger, garlic, mustard and reserved apricot juice; add pork. Seal bag and turn to coat; refrigerate for at least 1 hour.

2 Drain and discard marinade. In a large skillet or wok, stir-fry pork for 4-5 minutes or until juices run clear. Prepare salad mixes according to package directions; top with apricots and pork.

YIELD: 4 SERVINGS.

ground beef a la king

PREP/TOTAL TIME: 30 MIN.

1 package (10 ounces) frozen puff pastry shells
1 pound fresh baby carrots, cut in half
1-1/4 cups water, divided
1-1/2 pounds lean ground beef (90% lean)
1 package (8 ounces) sliced baby
   portobello mushrooms
2 tablespoons chopped shallots
3 tablespoons all-purpose flour
1 can (10-1/2 ounces) condensed
   beef broth, undiluted
1/4 cup tomato paste
1/4 cup dry red wine
1 tablespoon minced fresh tarragon
1/2 teaspoon salt
1/4 teaspoon pepper

1 Bake pastry shells according to package directions. In a microwave-safe bowl, combine the carrots and 1 cup of water. Cover and microwave on high for 8-10 minutes or until crisp-tender.

2 Meanwhile, in a large skillet, cook the beef, mushrooms and shallots over medium heat until meat is no longer pink; drain. Combine flour and broth until smooth. Add the broth mixture, tomato paste, wine, tarragon, salt, pepper and remaining water to beef mixture. Bring to a boil; cook and stir for 2 minutes or until thickened.

3 Drain carrots; add to skillet. Bring to a boil. Reduce heat; cover and simmer for 15 minutes. Remove top of pastry shells; fill with beef mixture.

YIELD: 6 SERVINGS.

EDITOR'S NOTE: This recipe was tested in a 1,100-watt microwave.

broccoli chicken casserole

PREP: 15 MIN. BAKE: 35 MIN.

I came across this recipe when I was in high school, and it's been a favorite ever since. Basil gives this casserole wonderful flavor. No one will know it's good for them!

Sharie Blevins • Chisholm, MN

2-1/2 cups uncooked yolk-free noodles

2-1/2 cups cubed cooked chicken breast

4 cups frozen broccoli florets, thawed

1 small onion, chopped

1 can (10-3/4 ounces) reduced-fat reduced-sodium condensed cream of chicken soup, undiluted

1/2 cup fat-free milk

1/2 cup shredded part-skim mozzarella cheese

1 teaspoon dried basil

1/4 teaspoon salt

1/8 teaspoon pepper

Paprika, optional

1 Cook noodles according to package directions; drain and place in a large bowl. Add the chicken, broccoli and onion. In a small bowl, combine the soup, milk, cheese, basil, salt and pepper. Pour over chicken mixture and stir until combined.

2 Transfer to a 2-qt. baking dish coated with cooking spray. Cover and bake at 350° for 35-40 minutes or until bubbly. Sprinkle with paprika if desired.

YIELD: 5 SERVINGS.

Between working full-time, going to school and raising three children, finding time-saving recipes that my family will eat is one of my biggest challenges. These pizzas take very little work and pack a huge amount of flavor.

Amy Grim • Chillicothe, OH

garlic toast pizzas

PREP/TOTAL TIME: 10 MIN.

1 package (11-1/4 ounces) frozen garlic bread, thawed

1/2 cup pizza sauce

1 package (3-1/2 ounces) sliced pepperoni

2 cups (8 ounces) shredded part-skim mozzarella cheese

1 Place the garlic bread in a foil-lined 15-in. x 10-in. x 1-in. baking pan. Spread with pizza sauce; top with pepperoni and cheese. Broil 3-4 in. from the heat for 4-6 minutes or until cheese is melted.

YIELD: 8 SLICES.

dishing out

When taking food to a potluck, welcoming a new family or bringing meals to someone, use dishes purchased at yard sales. This way you'll never feel bad if the dishes are lost, broken or not returned.

sausage mushroom pie

PREP: 20 MIN. BAKE: 40 MIN.

1 pound bulk pork sausage

1/4 cup chopped onion

2 packages (10 ounces each) frozen chopped spinach, thawed and squeezed dry

2 cans (8 ounces each) mushroom stems and pieces, drained

2 eggs, lightly beaten

3 cups (12 ounces) shredded part-skim mozzarella cheese

1 unbaked deep-dish pastry shell (9 inches)

1 cup (4 ounces) shredded cheddar cheese

1 In a large skillet, cook sausage and onion over medium heat until meat is no longer pink; drain. Stir in spinach and mushrooms. Combine eggs and mozzarella cheese; fold into sausage mixture. Spoon into pastry shell.

2 Cover and bake at 400° for 30 minutes. Uncover; sprinkle with cheddar cheese. Bake 10-15 minutes longer or until a knife inserted near the center comes out clean.

YIELD: 6-8 SERVINGS.

sweet-and-sour meatballs

PREP/TOTAL TIME: 30 MIN.

1 can (20 ounces) unsweetened pineapple chunks
1 package (12 ounces) frozen fully cooked homestyle meatballs, thawed
1 large green pepper, cut inot 1-inch pieces
3 tablespoons cornstarch
1/3 cup cold water
3 tablespoons cider vinegar
1 tablespoon soy sauce
1/2 cup packed brown sugar
Hot cooked rice, optional

1 Drain pineapple, reserving juice. Set pineapple aside. Add enough water to juice if needed to measure 1 cup. In a large skillet over medium heat, cook the meatballs, green pepper and juice mixture until heated through.

2 In a small bowl, combine the cornstarch with, cold water, vinegar and soy sauce until smooth. Add brown sugar and reserved pineapple to the pan; stir in cornstarch mixture. Bring to a boil; cook and stir for 2 minutes or until thickened. Serve with rice if desired .

YIELD: 6 SERVINGS.

My family loves this rich-tasting pasta as a main course or side dish. As long as the kids don't realize it contains squash, they'll keep on eating it!

Debbie Amacher
Amherst, NY

colorful mac 'n' cheese

PREP/TOTAL TIME: 25 MIN.

1-1/2 cups uncooked elbow macaroni
2 cups chopped zucchini
1/2 cup chopped onion
2 tablespoons canola oil
1 can (14-1/2 ounces) diced tomatoes, drained
1 can (10-3/4 ounces) condensed cheddar cheese soup, undiluted
2 cups (8 ounces) shredded cheddar cheese
1/2 cup milk
1/2 teaspoon dried basil
1/2 teaspoon prepared mustard

1 Cook macaroni according to package directions. Meanwhile, in a large saucepan, saute zucchini and onion in oil until tender. Stir in the tomatoes, soup, cheese, milk, basil and mustard.

2 Cook, uncovered, over medium heat for 6-7 minutes or until cheese is melted, stirring often. Drain macaroni; toss with vegetable cheese sauce.

YIELD: 4 SERVINGS.

These slow cooker recipes are perfect for creating a quick meal, because most of them have a preparation time of 20 minutes or less!

slow cooker cuisine

raspberry fondue dip

PREP/TOTAL TIME: 25 MIN.

1 package (10 ounces) frozen sweetened raspberries
1 cup apple butter
1 tablespoon red-hot candies
2 teaspoons cornstarch
Assorted fresh fruit

1 Place raspberries in a small bowl; set aside to thaw. Strain raspberries, reserving 1 tablespoon juice; discard seeds.

2 In a small saucepan, combine the strained berries, apple butter and red-hots; cook over medium heat until candies are dissolved, stirring occasionally.

3 In a small bowl, combine cornstarch and reserved juice until smooth; stir into berry mixture. Bring to a boil; cook and stir over medium heat for 1-2 minutes or until thickened. Serve warm or cold with fruit.

YIELD: 1 CUP.

yummy dippers

There are all kinds of delicious items you can use as dippers to serve with the Raspberry Fondue Dip. Try pretzel rods or mini pretzels, pieces of store-bought pound cake or chocolate and vanilla wafer cookies.

A little mango chutney goes a long way in giving a tasty twist to chicken. I even add a little curry powder to the dish for extra flavor.

Carol Conrad
Edmonton, AB

sweet 'n' sour curry chicken

PREP: 15 MIN. COOK: 4 HOURS

1 pound boneless skinless chicken breasts,
  cut into 1-inch pieces
1 can (14-1/2 ounces) stewed tomatoes, cut up
1 large green pepper, cut into 1-inch pieces
1 large onion, sliced
1/2 cup mango chutney
1-1/2 teaspoons curry powder
2 tablespoons cornstarch
1/4 cup water

1 In a 3-qt. slow cooker, combine the chicken, tomatoes, green pepper, onion, chutney and curry powder. Cover and cook on low for 4 hours or until chicken is no longer pink.

2 Combine cornstarch and water until smooth; stir into slow cooker. Cover and cook on high for 30 minutes or until thickened.

YIELD: 4 SERVINGS.

beef vegetable soup

PREP: 10 MIN. COOK: 4 HOURS

1 pound lean ground beef (90% lean)
1 medium onion, chopped
2 garlic cloves, minced
4 cups spicy hot V8 juice
2 cups coleslaw mix
1 can (14-1/2 ounces) Italian stewed tomatoes
1 package (10 ounces) frozen corn
1 package (9 ounces) frozen cut green beans
2 tablespoons Worcestershire sauce
1 teaspoon dried basil
1/4 teaspoon pepper

1 In a large nonstick skillet, cook beef and onion over medium heat until meat is no longer pink. Add garlic; cook 1 minute longer. Drain. Transfer to a 5-qt. slow cooker. Stir in the remaining ingredients. Cover and cook on high for 4-5 hours or until heated through.

YIELD: 9 SERVINGS.

saucy pork and beans

PREP: 15 MIN. COOK: 3 HOURS

Here's a robust side dish that easily comes together in the slow cooker. It's an excellent recipe for picnics and church socials.

Ginnie Busam • Pewee Valley, KY

4 cans (15 ounces each) pork and beans
8 bacon strips, cooked and crumbled
1 medium onion, chopped
1 small green pepper, chopped
3/4 cup cola
1/2 cup packed brown sugar
1/2 cup spicy brown mustard
1/2 cup ketchup
1/2 cup barbecue sauce

1 In a 5-qt. slow cooker, combine all ingredients. Cover and cook on high for 3-4 hours or until heated through. Serve with a slotted spoon.

YIELD: 12 SERVINGS.

Barbecued ribs are the perfect comfort food. Balsamic vinegar and Worcestershire sauce add zip to this recipe that is sure to satisfy!

Rebecca Knode
Mechanicsburg, PA

barbecue country ribs

PREP: 15 MIN. COOK: 6 HOURS

4 pounds boneless country-style pork ribs
1 bottle (12 ounces) chili sauce
1 cup ketchup
1/2 cup packed brown sugar
1/3 cup balsamic vinegar
2 tablespoons Worcestershire sauce
2 teaspoons onion powder
1 teaspoon salt
1 teaspoon garlic powder
1 teaspoon chili powder
1 teaspoon pepper
1/2 teaspoon hot pepper sauce, optional
1/4 teaspoon Liquid Smoke, optional

1 Place ribs in a 5-qt. slow cooker. Combine the chili sauce, ketchup, brown sugar, vinegar, Worcestershire sauce, seasonings, hot pepper sauce and Liquid Smoke if desired; pour over ribs.

2 Cover and cook on low for 6-7 hours or until meat is tender.

YIELD: 10 SERVINGS.

This hearty egg and potato recipe is a wonderful treat to take to a covered dish event or a morning get-together.

Barb Keith
Eau Claire, WI

hash brown egg brunch

PREP: 20 MIN. COOK: 4 HOURS

- 1 package (32 ounces) frozen shredded hash brown potatoes
- 1 pound bacon strips, cooked and crumbled
- 1 medium onion, chopped
- 1 medium green pepper, chopped
- 1-1/2 cups (6 ounces) shredded cheddar cheese
- 12 eggs
- 1 cup whole milk
- 1/2 teaspoon salt
- 1/2 teaspoon pepper

1 Layer a third of the potatoes, bacon, onion, green pepper and cheese in a 5-qt. slow cooker coated with cooking spray. Repeat the layers twice. In a large bowl, whisk the eggs, milk, salt and pepper; pour over the top.

2 Cover and cook on high for 30 minutes. Reduce heat to low; cook for 3-1/2 to 4 hours or until a thermometer reads 160°.

YIELD: 10 SERVINGS.

onion meat loaf

PREP: 10 MIN. COOK: 5 HOURS

My husband and I really enjoy this delicious meat loaf. I use just five ingredients to assemble the easy entree before popping it in the slow cooker.

Rhonda Cowden • Quincy, IL

2 eggs
1/2 cup ketchup
3/4 cup quick-cooking oats
1 envelope onion soup mix
2 pounds ground beef

1 In a large bowl, combine the eggs, ketchup, oats and soup mix. Crumble beef over mixture; mix well. Shape into a round loaf.

2 Cut three 20-in. x 3-in. strips of heavy-duty aluminum foil. Crisscross the strips so they resemble the spokes of a wheel. Place meat loaf in the center of the strips; pull the strips up and bend the edges to form handles. Grasp the foil handles to transfer loaf to a 3-qt. slow cooker. (Leave the foil in while meat loaf cooks.)

3 Cover and cook on low for 5-6 hours or until no pink remains and a meat thermometer reaches 160°. Using foil strips, lift meat loaf out of slow cooker.

YIELD: 8 SERVINGS.

These appetizers vanish in minutes whenever I serve them, so I usually double the recipe and use my larger slow cooker.
Andrea Chamberlain • Macedon, NY

meat loaf tip

Select ground beef that is bright red in a tightly sealed package. Purchase all ground beef before the "sell by" date. Handle the mixture as little as possible when shaping the meat loaf to keep the final product light in texture.

mini hot dogs 'n' meatballs

PREP: 5 MIN. COOK: 3 HOURS

1 package (12 ounces) frozen fully cooked Italian meatballs
1 package (16 ounces) miniature hot dogs or smoked sausages
1 package (3-1/2 ounces) sliced pepperoni
1 jar (26 ounces) meatless spaghetti sauce
1 bottle (18 ounces) barbecue sauce
1 bottle (12 ounces) chili sauce

1 In a 5-qt. slow cooker, combine all ingredients. Cover and cook on low for 3 hours or until heated through.

YIELD: 8 CUPS.

On hot summer days, this recipe cooks without heating up the kitchen, while I work on the rest of the meal. It's easy to double or triple for crowds, and if there is extra, you can freeze it to enjoy later!

Carol Losier
Baldwinsville, NY

slow cooker sloppy joes

PREP: 20 MIN. COOK: 3 HOURS

1-1/2 pounds ground beef
1 cup chopped celery
1/2 cup chopped onion
1 bottle (12 ounces) chili sauce
2 tablespoons brown sugar
2 tablespoons sweet pickle relish
1 tablespoon Worcestershire sauce
1 teaspoon salt
1/8 teaspoon pepper
8 hamburger buns, split

1 In a large skillet, cook the beef, celery and onion over medium heat until meat is no longer pink; drain. Transfer to a 3-qt. slow cooker.

2 Stir in the chili sauce, brown sugar, pickle relish, Worcestershire sauce, salt and pepper. Cover and cook on low for 3-4 hours or until the flavors are combined. Spoon 1/2 cup of the beef mixture onto each bun.

YIELD: 8 SERVINGS.

pizza dip

PREP: 10 MIN. COOK: 1-1/2 HOURS

2 packages (8 ounces each) cream cheese, cubed

1 can (15 ounces) pizza sauce

1 package (8 ounces) sliced pepperoni, chopped

1 can (3.8 ounces) chopped ripe olives, drained

2 cups (8 ounces) shredded part-skim mozzarella cheese

Bagel chips or garlic toast

1 Place the cream cheese in a 3-qt. slow cooker. Combine the pizza sauce, pepperoni and olives; pour over cream cheese. Top with mozzarella cheese. Cover and cook on low for 1-1/2 to 2 hours or until cheese is melted. Stir; serve warm with bagel chips or garlic toast.

YIELD: 5-1/2 CUPS.

brisket with cranberry gravy

PREP: 25 MIN. COOK: 8 HOURS

1 fresh beef brisket (2-1/2 pounds)
1/2 teaspoon salt
1/4 teaspoon pepper
1 can (14 ounces) whole-berry cranberry sauce
1 can (8 ounces) tomato sauce
1/2 cup chopped onion
1 tablespoon prepared mustard

1 Rub brisket with salt and pepper; place in a 5-qt. slow cooker. Combine the cranberry sauce, tomato sauce, onion and mustard; pour over brisket.

2 Cover and cook on low for 8-10 hours or until meat is tender. Remove brisket; thinly slice across the grain. Skim fat from cooking juices; serve with brisket.

YIELD: 6-8 SERVINGS.

EDITOR'S NOTE: This is a fresh beef brisket, not corned beef.

I get this satisfying sausage-and-bean stew started in the slow cooker, then spend the afternoon curled up with a good book. It's an effortless meal that tastes great.

Glenda Holmes
Riley, KS

smoky bean stew

PREP: 10 MIN. COOK: 4 HOURS

1 package (16 ounces) miniature smoked sausage links
1 can (16 ounces) baked beans
2 cups frozen cut green beans
2 cups frozen lima beans
1/2 cup packed brown sugar

1/2 cup thinly sliced fresh carrots
1/2 cup chopped onion
1/2 cup ketchup
1 tablespoon cider vinegar
1 teaspoon prepared mustard

1 In a 3-qt. slow cooker, combine all ingredients. Cover and cook on high for 4-5 hours or until vegetables are tender.

YIELD: 6-8 SERVINGS.

italian chicken

PREP: 20 MIN. COOK: 3 HOURS

6 boneless skinless chicken breast halves
(about 8 ounces each)

1 can (14-1/2 ounces) Italian stewed tomatoes

3/4 cup plus 3 tablespoons water, divided

2 tablespoons dried minced onion

2 teaspoons chicken bouillon granules

2 teaspoons chili powder

1/2 teaspoon dried tarragon

1/2 teaspoon Italian seasoning

1/4 teaspoon garlic powder

3 tablespoons cornstarch

Hot cooked rice

1 Place chicken in a 5-qt. slow cooker. In a small bowl, combine the tomatoes, 3/4 cup water, onion, bouillon and seasonings; pour over chicken. Cover and cook on low for 3-4 hours or until a meat thermometer reads 170°.

2 Transfer chicken to a serving platter; keep warm. Skim fat from cooking juices; transfer to a small saucepan. Bring liquid to a boil. Combine cornstarch and remaining water until smooth. Gradually stir into the pan. Bring to a boil; cook and stir for 2 minutes or until thickened. Serve with chicken and rice.

YIELD: 6 SERVINGS.

When my husband and I were both working full-time, we loved this recipe's 81/2-hour cook time. The beef brisket tastes so good after simmering all day in the slow cooker. The cinnamon and chili sauce add a unique touch to the gravy.

Anna Stodolak
Volant, PA

slow-cooked beef brisket

PREP: 10 MIN. COOK: 8-1/2 HOURS

1 large onion, sliced
1 fresh beef brisket (3 to 4 pounds), cut in half
1/4 teaspoon pepper
1 jar (4-1/2 ounces) sliced mushrooms, drained
3/4 cup beef broth
1/2 cup chili sauce
1/4 cup packed brown sugar
2 garlic cloves, minced
1/4 cup all-purpose flour
1/4 cup cold water

1 Place onion in a 5-qt. slow cooker. Rub brisket with pepper; place over onion. Top with mushrooms. In a bowl, combine the broth, chili sauce, brown sugar and garlic; pour over brisket. Cover and cook on low for 8-9 hours or until meat is tender.

2 Remove brisket and keep warm. In a small bowl, combine flour and water until smooth; stir into cooking juices. Cover and cook on high for 30 minutes or until thickened. Slice brisket; serve with gravy.

YIELD: 6-8 SERVINGS.

EDITOR'S NOTE: This is a fresh beef brisket, not corned beef.

I trim the meat, cut up
the vegetables and
store them in separate
containers the night before.
The next day, I can toss
all of the ingredients into
the slow cooker in minutes.
Shortly before dinnertime,
I cook the noodles and bake
some cheesy garlic toast
to complete the meal.

Mary Jo Miller
Mansfield, OH

beef burgundy

PREP: 10 MIN. COOK: 5-1/2 HOURS

1-1/2 pounds beef stew meat, cut into
   1-inch cubes

1/2 pound whole fresh mushrooms, halved

4 medium carrots, chopped

1 can (10-3/4 ounces) condensed golden
   mushroom soup, undiluted

1 large onion, cut into thin wedges

1/2 cup Burgundy wine or beef broth

1/4 cup quick-cooking tapioca

1/2 teaspoon salt

1/4 teaspoon dried thyme

1/4 teaspoon pepper

Hot cooked egg noodles

1 In a 5-qt. slow cooker, combine beef, mushrooms,
carrots, soup, onion, wine, tapioca, salt, thyme and
pepper. Cover; cook on low for 5-1/2 to 6-1/2 hours
or until the meat is tender. Serve with noodles.

YIELD: 6 SERVINGS.

seasoned pork sandwiches

PREP: 20 MIN. COOK: 5 HOURS

This is one of those dishes that my husband never seems to get tired of. The bonus for me is that it's quick, easy to make and even easier to clean up!

Jacque Thompson • Houston, TX

1 boneless whole pork loin roast (2 to 3 pounds)
1 tablespoon fajita seasoning mix
1/4 teaspoon garlic powder
1/2 cup Italian salad dressing
1/4 cup Worcestershire sauce
8 sandwich rolls, split

1 Cut roast in half; place in a 5-qt. slow cooker. Sprinkle with fajita seasoning and garlic powder. Pour salad dressing and Worcestershire sauce over meat. Cover and cook on low for 5-6 hours or until tender.

2 Remove roast; shred meat with two forks. Return to cooking juices; heat through. Using a slotted spoon, serve pork on rolls.

YIELD: 8 SERVINGS.

It takes only minutes to ready this round steak for the slow cooker, then it simmers most of the day to a tasty tenderness. The flavorful beef strips and sauce are also nice over hot rice.

Linda Bloom • McHenry, IL

round steak sauerbraten

PREP: 20 MIN. COOK: 7 HOURS

1 envelope brown gravy mix
2 tablespoons plus 1-1/2 teaspoons brown sugar
2-1/2 cups cold water, divided
1 cup chopped onion
2 tablespoons white vinegar
2 teaspoons Worcestershire sauce
4 bay leaves
2-1/2 pounds boneless beef top round steak, cut into 3-inch x 1/2-inch strips
2 teaspoons salt
1 teaspoon pepper
1/4 cup cornstarch
10 cups hot cooked egg noodles

1 In a 5-qt. slow cooker, combine the gravy mix, brown sugar, 2 cups water, onion, vinegar, Worcestershire sauce and bay leaves.

2 Sprinkle the beef with the salt and pepper; stir into gravy mixture. Cover and cook on low for 6-1/2 to 7 hours or until meat is tender.

3 Combine cornstarch and remaining water until smooth; stir into beef mixture. Cover and cook on high for 30 minutes or until thickened. Discard bay leaves. Serve with noodles.

YIELD: 10 SERVINGS.

herbed beef
with noodles

PREP: 25 MIN. COOK: 5 HOURS

2 pounds boneless beef top round steak

1/2 teaspoon salt

1/2 teaspoon pepper, divided

2 teaspoons canola oil

1 can (10-3/4 ounces) reduced-fat reduced-sodium condensed cream of celery soup, undiluted

1 medium onion, chopped

1 tablespoon fat-free milk

1 teaspoon dried oregano

1/2 teaspoon dried thyme

6 cups cooked wide egg noodles

Chopped celery leaves, optional

1 Cut steak into serving-size pieces; sprinkle with salt and 1/4 teaspoon pepper. In a large nonstick skillet coated with cooking spray, brown meat in oil on both sides. Transfer to a 3-qt. slow cooker.

2 In a small bowl, combine the soup, onion, milk, oregano, thyme and remaining pepper. Pour over meat. Cover and cook on low for 5-6 hours or until meat is tender. Serve with noodles. Sprinkle with celery leaves if desired.

YIELD: 8 SERVINGS.

scalloped taters

PREP: 10 MIN. COOK: 4-1/2 HOURS

1 package (2 pounds) frozen cubed hash brown potatoes

1 can (10-3/4 ounces) condensed cream of chicken soup, undiluted

1-1/2 cups whole milk

1 cup (4 ounces) shredded cheddar cheese

1/2 cup plus 1 tablespoon butter, melted, divided

1/4 cup dried minced onion

1/2 teaspoon salt

1/8 teaspoon pepper

3/4 cup crushed cornflakes

1 In a large bowl, combine the hash browns, soup, milk, cheese, 1/2 cup melted butter, onion, salt and pepper. Pour into a greased 5-qt. slow cooker. Cover and cook on low for 4-1/2 to 5 hours or until potatoes are tender.

2 Just before serving, combine the cornflake crumbs and remaining melted butter in a pie plate. Bake at 350° for 4-6 minutes or until golden brown. Stir the potatoes; sprinkle with crumb topping.

YIELD: 12 SERVINGS.

Decadent dinner finales don't have to take all day to prepare. These simple-to-make sensations will leave a sweet impression on family and friends.

delectable desserts

pineapple-caramel sponge cakes

PREP/TOTAL TIME: 10 MIN.

1 can (8 ounces) unsweetened crushed pineapple, drained
1/2 cup caramel ice cream topping
4 individual round sponge cakes
1 pint vanilla ice cream, softened

1 In a small saucepan, combine pineapple and caramel topping. Cook over medium heat for 2-3 minutes or until heated through, stirring occasionally.

2 Place sponge cakes on dessert plates. Top each with a scoop of ice cream and 1/4 cup pineapple sauce. Serve immediately.

YIELD: 4 SERVINGS.

peach almond bars

PREP: 25 MIN. BAKE: 20 MIN. + COOLING

1 tube (16-1/2 ounces) refrigerated sugar
   cookie dough
1 jar (18 ounces) peach preserves
1-1/2 cups slivered almonds, divided
4 egg whites
1/2 cup sugar

1 Let dough stand at room temperature for 5-10
minutes to soften. Press into an ungreased 13-in.
x 9-in. baking pan. Bake at 350° for 12-15 minutes
or until golden brown.

2 Spread preserves over crust. Sprinkle with 3/4
cup almonds. In a large bowl, beat egg whites on
medium speed until soft peaks form. Gradually
beat in sugar, 1 tablespoon at a time, on high until
stiff glossy peaks form and sugar is dissolved.

3 Spread meringue evenly over almonds. Sprinkle
with remaining almonds. Bake at 350° for 20-25
minutes or until lightly browned. Cool on a wire
rack. Store in the refrigerator.

YIELD: 2 DOZEN.

raisin pecan baklava

PREP: 30 MIN. BAKE: 20 MIN. + COOLING

1/3 cup sugar
1/4 cup water
3 tablespoons honey
4-1/2 teaspoons lemon juice
1/2 cup chopped pecans, toasted
1/2 cup Grape-Nuts
1/2 cup raisins
1/3 cup packed brown sugar
1/2 teaspoon ground cinnamon
8 sheets phyllo dough (14 inches x 9 inches)

1 In a small saucepan, combine the sugar, water, honey and lemon juice. Bring to a boil; cook and stir until sugar is dissolved. Remove from the heat.

2 In a small bowl, combine the pecans, cereal, raisins, brown sugar and cinnamon. Stir in 3 tablespoons of honey mixture; set aside.

3 Stack phyllo sheets on a work surface; trim 1 in. from the 9-in. side. Cut in half lengthwise, forming 8-in. x 7-in. rectangles. (Keep remaining phyllo covered with plastic wrap and a damp towel to prevent it from drying out.) Overlap two pieces in a greased 8-in. square baking dish; spray with cooking spray. Repeat three times.

4 Spread nut mixture over top. Overlap two pieces of phyllo to cover nut mixture; spray with cooking spray. Repeat with remaining phyllo. Using a sharp knife, cut into 24 rectangles, about 2-1/2 in. x 1 in.

5 Bake, uncovered, at 350° for 20-25 minutes or until golden brown. Reheat reserved honey mixture; pour over hot baklava. Cool completely on a wire rack.

YIELD: 2 DOZEN.

raspberry cheesecake pie

PREP: 25 MIN. BAKE: 25 MIN. + CHILLING

- 2 packages (8 ounces each) cream cheese, softened
- 1/2 cup sugar
- 1/2 teaspoon vanilla extract
- 2 eggs
- 1 chocolate crumb crust (8 inches)
- 1-1/2 teaspoons unflavored gelatin
- 2 tablespoons cold water
- 1/2 cup seedless raspberry jam
- 1 cup heavy whipping cream
- 2 tablespoons confectioners' sugar

1 In a large bowl, beat the cream cheese, sugar and vanilla until smooth. Add eggs; beat on low speed just until combined. Pour into crust.

Bake at 325° for 25-30 minutes or until the center is almost set. Cool on a wire rack for 1 hour. Refrigerate overnight.

2 In a small saucepan, sprinkle gelatin over cold water; let stand for 1 minute. Cook over low heat, stirring until gelatin is completely dissolved. Stir in jam. Refrigerate for 10 minutes.

3 In small bowl, beat cream until it begins to thicken. Gradually add confectioners' sugar; beat until stiff peaks form. Remove 1/2 cup for garnish; cover and refrigerate.

4 Gently stir 3/4 cup whipped cream into raspberry mixture just until blended. Fold in the remaining whipped cream; spread over cheesecake. Refrigerate for at least 1 hour. Garnish with reserved whipped cream.

YIELD: 6-8 SERVINGS.

My great-grandmother used to make this cake, which has been a family favorite for years. You won't believe it starts with a cake mix! Lemon pudding and apricot nectar make it especially tangy and moist. It's delicious plain or served with ice cream or whipped cream.

Gail Mast
Clarkson, KY

fluted lemon cake

PREP: 15 MIN. BAKE: 45 MIN. + COOLING

1 package (18-1/4 ounces) yellow cake mix

1 package (3.4 ounces) instant lemon pudding mix

1 cup apricot nectar

1/2 cup canola oil

4 eggs

1 teaspoon lemon extract

LEMON GLAZE:

1 cup confectioners' sugar

2 tablespoons lemon juice

1 In a large bowl, combine the cake and dry pudding mixes, apricot nectar, oil, eggs and lemon extract; beat on low for 30 seconds. Beat on medium speed for about 2 minutes. Pour into a greased and floured 10-in. fluted tube pan.

2 Bake at 350° for 45-55 minutes or until a toothpick inserted near the center comes out clean. Cool for 10 minutes before removing from pan to a wire rack to cool completely.

3 In a small bowl, combine glaze ingredients until smooth; drizzle over warm cake.

YIELD: 12 SERVINGS.

I originally whipped up these bars to bring something new and colorful to my Christmas cookie trays. I bake them ahead when convenient because they freeze well. You can use M&M's in different colors for holidays year-round.

Julie Wischmeier
Brownstown, IN

peanut butter s'mores bars

PREP: 10 MIN. BAKE: 20 MIN. + CHILLING

1 tube (16-1/2 ounces) refrigerated peanut butter cookie dough
3-1/2 cups miniature marshmallows
3/4 cup milk chocolate chips
2 teaspoons shortening
1-1/2 cups milk chocolate M&M's

1 Let the cookie dough stand at room temperature for 5-10 minutes to soften. Cut into 24 slices and arrange side by side in an ungreased 13-in. x 9-in. baking pan. Pat together to close gaps.

2 Bake at 350° for 18-20 minutes or until lightly browned and edges are firm. Sprinkle with marshmallows; bake 2-3 minutes longer or until marshmallows are puffy.

3 In a small microwave-safe bowl, melt chocolate chips and shortening; stir until smooth. Sprinkle M&M's over marshmallow layer; drizzle with melted chocolate. Chill until set before cutting.

YIELD: 2 DOZEN.

sugar cookie tarts

PREP/TOTAL TIME: 20 MIN. + CHILLING

5 tablespoons sugar, divided
1 teaspoon cornstarch
Dash salt
3 tablespoons water
2 tablespoons orange juice
1 tablespoon lemon juice
1 package (3 ounces) cream cheese, softened
4 large sugar cookies (3 inches)
1 cup sliced assorted fresh fruit (strawberries, kiwifruit and/or bananas)

1 For the glaze, in a small saucepan, combine the 3 tablespoons sugar, cornstarch and salt. Gradually stir in the water, orange juice and lemon juice. Bring to a boil over medium heat; cook and stir for 2 minutes or until thickened. Remove from the heat; cool.

2 In a small bowl, beat cream cheese and remaining sugar until smooth. Spread over each cookie; arrange fruit on top. Drizzle with glaze. Refrigerate until chilled.

YIELD: 4 SERVINGS.

about bananas

If bananas are too green, place them in a paper bag until ripe. For storage, set ripe bananas in a tightly sealed plastic bag and refrigerate. The peel will become brown but the flesh will remain unchanged.

chocolate cherry cheesecake

PREP: 15 MIN. BAKE: 30 MIN. + COOLING

1 jar (12 ounces) maraschino cherries
2 packages (8 ounces each) cream cheese, softened
1/2 cup sugar
2 eggs
1/2 cup miniature semisweet chocolate chips
1 chocolate cookie crust (9 inches)
6 chocolate-covered cherries

1 Drain maraschino cherries, reserving 2 teaspoons juice. Cut cherries into quarters; set aside.

2 In a small bowl, beat the cream cheese, sugar and reserved cherry juice until smooth. Add eggs; beat just until combined. Fold in chocolate chips and reserved cherries.

3 Pour into crust (crust will be full). Bake at 350° for 30-35 minutes or until center is almost set. Cool on a wire rack. Serve with chocolate-covered cherries.

YIELD: 6 SERVINGS.

white chocolate dream torte

PREP/TOTAL TIME: 25 MIN. + CHILLING

1 package (8 ounces) cream cheese, softened
1/3 cup sugar
4 ounces white baking chocolate, melted and cooled
1-1/2 teaspoons vanilla extract, divided
1 carton (16 ounces) frozen whipped topping, thawed, divided
2 packages (3 ounces each) ladyfingers, split
3/4 cup white baking chips

1 In a large bowl, beat cream cheese and sugar until smooth. Beat in melted white chocolate and 1 teaspoon vanilla. Fold in half of the whipped topping.

2 Arrange ladyfingers on the bottom and around the edge of an ungreased 9-in. springform pan. Spread half of the cream cheese mixture evenly over ladyfingers on bottom of pan. Arrange remaining ladyfingers over cream cheese mixture to resemble the spokes of a wheel. Sprinkle with white chips.

3 Spread with remaining cream cheese mixture. Combine remaining whipped topping and vanilla; spread over the top. Cover and refrigerate for at least 2 hours. Remove sides of pan before slicing.

YIELD: 12 SERVINGS.

caramel chocolate fondue

PREP/TOTAL TIME: 15 MIN.

2 packages (5-1/2 ounces each) Riesen's chewy chocolate-covered caramels

1/2 cup heavy whipping cream

1 teaspoon rum extract

Cubed pound cake, sliced bananas and fresh strawberries

1 cup nut topping, optional

1 In a heavy saucepan, melt caramels with cream over low heat, stirring frequently until smooth. Remove from the heat. Stir in extract.

2 Keep warm. Dip cake and fruit into fondue, then into nut topping if desired.

YIELD: 1-1/2 CUPS.

These rich cookies make baking easy because they rely on convenience products I keep on hand.
— Sarah Vasques
Milford, NH

candy cookie cups

PREP: 15 MIN. BAKE: 15 MIN. + COOLING

1/2 cup finely chopped macadamia nuts
1 package (16 ounces) individually portioned refrigerated white chip macadamia nut cookie dough
24 miniature peanut butter cups

1 Sprinkle macadamia nuts into 24 greased miniature muffin cups, 1 teaspoon in each. Cut each portion of cookie dough in half; place each half in a muffin cup.

2 Bake at 325° for 11-13 minutes or until golden brown. Immediately place a peanut butter cup in each cookie; press down gently. Cool completely before removing from pans to wire racks.

YIELD: 2 DOZEN.

peanut butter delights

PREP/TOTAL TIME: 30 MIN.

With refrigerated cookie dough, these tasty treats could not be quicker. Everyone loves them.

Janice Rasmussen • Atlantic, IA

1 package (16 ounces) refrigerated ready-to-bake peanut butter cookies with candy pieces
2 tablespoons creamy peanut butter
3 ounces milk chocolate candy coating, melted

1 Bake cookies according to package directions. Cool on wire racks. Spread 12 cookies with 1/2 teaspoon peanut butter each; spoon melted chocolate over peanut butter. Let stand for 5 minutes or until set. Save remaining cookies for another use.

YIELD: 1 DOZEN.

chocolate-peanut butter cookies

PREP: 15 MIN. BAKE: 10 MIN./BATCH

2 cans (16 ounces each) chocolate fudge frosting, divided
1 egg
1 cup chunky peanut butter
1-1/2 cups all-purpose flour
Granulated sugar

1 Set aside one can plus 1/3 cup frosting. In a large bowl, combine the egg, peanut butter and remaining frosting. Stir in flour just until moistened.

2 Drop by rounded tablespoonfuls 2 in. apart on baking sheets coated with cooking spray. Flatten cookies with a fork dipped in sugar.

3 Bake at 375° for 8-11 minutes or until set. Remove to wire racks. Cool completely; spread with reserved frosting.

YIELD: 3-1/2 DOZEN.

flatten faster

To quickly flatten these cookies, use the grid end of a meat mallet, instead of a fork. First press the end of the meat mallet into the sugar to avoid the dough from sticking.

sorbet cream puffs

PREP/TOTAL TIME: 10 MIN.

  1 cup mixed fresh berries
  1 tablespoon sugar
  2 cups peach sorbet
  4 cream puff shells
  Whipped cream

1 In a small bowl, combine berries and sugar. Place a scoop of sorbet in each cream puff shell; dollop with whipped cream. Replace tops. Serve immediately with berry mixture.

YIELD: 4 SERVINGS.

pineapple sour cream pie

PREP/TOTAL TIME: 5 MIN. + CHILLING

Canned pineapple and instant pudding make it a snap to prepare this no-bake pie that gets its richness from a container of sour cream.

Jaye Bloomer • Canoga Park, CA

  1 package (3.4 ounces) instant vanilla pudding mix
  2 cups (16 ounces) sour cream
  1 can (8 ounces) crushed pineapple, undrained
  1 graham cracker crust (9 inches)
  Whipped cream, optional

1 In a small bowl, combine the pudding mix and sour cream. Stir in the pineapple. Spread into crust. Cover and refrigerate for 3 hours or until set. Serve with whipped cream if desired.

YIELD: 6-8 SERVINGS.

chocolate mint cream cake

PREP: 30 MIN. BAKE: 20 MIN. + COOLING

1 package (18-1/4 ounces) white cake mix

1 cup water

1/2 cup canola oil

3 eggs

1/2 teaspoon peppermint extract

1 cup crushed mint cream-filled chocolate sandwich cookies

TOPPING:

2 packages (3.9 ounces each) instant chocolate pudding mix

1/3 cup confectioners' sugar

1-1/2 cups cold whole milk

1/2 to 1 teaspoon peppermint extract

1 carton (12 ounces) frozen whipped topping, thawed

1/2 cup crushed mint cream-filled chocolat sandwich cookies

15 mint Andes candies

1 In a large bowl, combine the cake mix, water, oil, eggs and peppermint extract; beat on low speed for about 30 seconds. Beat on medium speed for about 2 minutes. Fold in crushed cookies.

2 Pour into three greased and floured 9-in. round baking pans. Bake at 350° for 18-24 minutes or until a toothpick inserted near the center comes out clean. Cool for 10 minutes before removing from pans to wire racks to cool completely.

3 For topping, combine the dry pudding mixes, confectioners' sugar, milk and extract until thickened. Fold in whipped topping and crushed cookies.

4 Place one cake layer on a serving plate; spread with topping. Repeat layers twice. Frost sides of cake with remaining topping.

5 Chop eight candies; sprinkle over center of cake. Cut remaining candies in half; garnish each serving with a half candy. Store in the refrigerator.

YIELD: 14 SERVINGS.

peach cheese pie

PREP/TOTAL TIME: 15 MIN. + CHILLING

1 can (15 ounces) sliced peaches in extra-light syrup
1/4 cup cold water
1 envelope unflavored gelatin
1 package (8 ounces) reduced-fat cream cheese, cubed
1/4 cup sugar
1 graham cracker crust (9 inches)
Fresh peach slices, optional

1 Drain peaches, reserving syrup; set peaches aside. In a small saucepan, combine water and reserved syrup; sprinkle with gelatin. Let stand for 1 minute. Heat over low heat, stirring until gelatin is completely dissolved, about 2 minutes. Cool slightly.

2 Transfer to a food processor. Add the peaches, cream cheese and sugar; cover and process until smooth. Pour into crust. Cover and refrigerate until set, about 1 hour. Refrigerate leftovers. Garnish with peach slices if desired.

YIELD: 8 SERVINGS.

strawberry-banana angel torte

PREP/TOTAL TIME: 20 MIN.

1 prepared angel food cake (8 to 10 ounces)
1/2 cup sour cream
1/4 cup sugar
1/4 cup pureed fresh strawberries
3/4 cup sliced ripe bananas
1/2 cup sliced fresh strawberries
1 cup heavy whipping cream, whipped
Halved fresh strawberries

1 Split cake horizontally into three layers; place bottom layer on a serving plate. In a large bowl, combine the sour cream, sugar and pureed strawberries; fold in bananas and sliced strawberries. Fold in whipped cream.

2 Spread a third of the filling between each layer; spread remaining filling over top. Cover and refrigerate until serving. Garnish with halved strawberries.

YIELD: 8-10 SERVINGS.

easy strawberry napoleons

PREP: 20 MIN. + CHILLING BAKE: 10 MIN. + COOLING

1 sheet puff pastry, thawed according to
  package directions
1 quart fresh strawberries, sliced
2 tablespoons sugar
1/4 teaspoon vanilla extract
1 cup cold whole milk
1 package (3.4 ounces) instant vanilla
  pudding mix
2 cups whipped topping
1/2 cup semisweet chocolate chips

1 Preheat oven to 400°. Unfold thawed puff pastry
  on cutting board. With a sharp knife, cut pastry
  into nine squares. Place on baking sheet coated
  with cooking spray. Bake 10-15 minutes or until
  golden brown. Remove from pan to wire rack
  to cool completely.

2 In a large bowl, combine the strawberries, sugar
  and vanilla; set aside. In another bowl, whisk
  milk and pudding mix for two minutes. Let stand
  for 2 minutes or until soft-set. Stir in whipped
  topping until thoroughly blended. Cover and
  refrigerate.

3 To assemble, split puff pastry squares horizontally
  for a total of 18 squares. Set aside six tops. Place
  six of the remaining puff pastry pieces on individual
  serving plates. Spread about 1/4 cup pudding
  mixture over each pastry square. Top with a
  spoonful of strawberries and another piece of
  puff pastry. Spread remaining pudding mixture
  over pastry pieces. Top with remaining strawberries
  and reserved pastry tops.

4 In a microwave, melt chocolate chips; stir until
  smooth. Transfer melted chocolate to a small
  plastic bag. Cut tiny corner from bag; squeeze
  chocolate over napoleons.

YIELD: 6 SERVINGS.

frozen peanut parfait pies

PREP/TOTAL TIME: 20 MIN. + FREEZING

1 package (8 ounces) cream cheese, softened
1 can (14 ounces) sweetened condensed milk
1 carton (16 ounces) frozen whipped topping, thawed
1 jar (11-3/4 ounces) hot fudge ice cream topping, warmed
2 cups dry roasted peanuts
2 pastry shells (9 inches), baked

1 In a large bowl, beat cream cheese and condensed milk until smooth; fold in whipped topping. Spread a fourth of the mixture into each pie shell. Drizzle each with a fourth of the fudge topping; sprinkle each with 1/2 cup peanuts. Repeat layers.

2 Cover and freeze for 4 hours or overnight. Remove from the freezer 5 minutes before cutting.

YIELD: 2 PIES (6-8 SERVINGS EACH).

peanut lover's pie

PREP/TOTAL TIME: 30 MIN. + FREEZING

- 6 tablespoons honey-roasted peanuts, divided
- 1-1/2 cups graham cracker crumbs
- 7 tablespoons butter, melted
- 3 pints chocolate ice cream, softened
- 1 cup plus 1 tablespoon peanut butter, divided
- 3/4 cup coarsely chopped peanut butter cups, divided
- 1/2 cup caramel ice cream topping

1 Chop 1 tablespoon of peanuts; set aside. Place the remaining peanuts in a food processor; cover and process until ground. In a small bowl, combine the ground nuts, cracker crumbs and butter. Press onto the bottom and up the sides of an ungreased 9-in. pie plate. Freeze until firm, about 30 minutes.

2 In a large bowl, combine the ice cream and 1 cup peanut butter until blended. Spoon half into crust.

Return remaining ice cream mixture to the freezer. Cover and freeze pie until almost firm, about 1 hour. Sprinkle with about two-thirds of the chopped peanut butter cups. Freeze for 30 minutes.

3 Meanwhile, resoften remaining ice cream mixture. Spread over peanut butter cups (pie will be very full). Cover and freeze for at least 2 hours or until almost firm. Sprinkle with chopped peanuts and remaining chopped peanut butter cups. Cover and freeze until firm, about 1 hour longer.

4 Remove from the freezer 15 minutes before serving. Combine caramel topping and remaining peanut butter; drizzle some over dessert plates. Top with a piece of pie; drizzle with remaining caramel mixture.

YIELD: 8 SERVINGS.

My mom made these dressy, sweet cookies for cookie exchanges when I was a little girl, and let me sprinkle on the almonds and coconut. They're so yummy and easy to fix that sometimes I can't wait until the holidays to bake a batch.

Dawn Burns
Troy, OH

caramel heavenlies

PREP: 20 MIN. BAKE: 15 MIN.

12 whole graham crackers
2 cups miniature marshmallows
3/4 cup butter
3/4 cup packed brown sugar
1 teaspoon ground cinnamon
1 teaspoon vanilla extract
1 cup sliced almonds
1 cup flaked coconut

1 Line a 15-in. x 10-in. x 1-in. baking pan with foil. Place graham crackers in pan; cover with marshmallows. In a saucepan over medium heat, cook and stir butter, brown sugar and cinnamon until the butter is melted and sugar is dissolved. Remove from the heat; stir in vanilla.

2 Spoon the butter mixture over the marshmallows. Sprinkle with the almonds and coconut. Bake at 350° for 14-16 minutes or until browned. Cool completely. Cut into 2-in. squares, then cut each square in half to form triangles.

YIELD: ABOUT 6 DOZEN.

fancy sugar cookie bars

PREP: 10 MIN. BAKE: 20 MIN. + COOLING

 1 tube (16-1/2 ounces) refrigerated sugar
   cookie dough
 1 cup semisweet chocolate chips
 1/2 cup flaked coconut
 1/4 cup chopped pecans

1 Let the dough stand at room temperature for
  5-10 minutes to soften. Press into an ungreased
  13-in. x 9-in. baking pan. Bake at 350° for 10-12
  minutes or until golden brown.

2 Sprinkle with chocolate chips, coconut and pecans.
  Bake 10-12 minutes longer or until golden brown.
  Cool on a wire rack.

  YIELD: 2 DOZEN.

cherry pie dessert

PREP: 20 MIN. BAKE: 20 MIN. + COOLING

A friend gave me this recipe. It's buttery, and crunchy — kids love it!

Alisha Rice • Albany, OR

 2 cups all-purpose flour
 1/2 cup confectioners' sugar
 1 cup cold butter, cubed
 1 can (30 ounces) cherry pie filling
 1 carton (12 ounces) frozen whipped
   topping, thawed

1 Combine flour and confectioners' sugar. Cut in
  butter until mixture resembles coarse crumbs. Press
  into an ungreased 13-in. x 9-in. baking dish.

2 Bake at 350° for 18-20 minutes or until lightly
  browned. Cool completely on a wire rack. Spoon
  pie filling over crust; spread with whipped topping.
  Store in the refrigerator.

  YIELD: 12-15 SERVINGS.

strawberry shortbread pie

PREP/TOTAL: 15 MIN. + CHILLING

3/4 cup sugar
3 tablespoons cornstarch
1-1/2 cups water
1 package (3 ounces) strawberry gelatin
4 cups sliced fresh strawberries
1 shortbread crust (9 inches)

1 In a small saucepan, combine the sugar, cornstarch and water until smooth. Bring to a boil; cook and stir for 2 minutes or until thickened. Remove from the heat; stir in gelatin powder until dissolved. Transfer to a small bowl. Chill until partially set.

2 Place strawberries in the crust; pour gelatin mixture over berries. Cover and refrigerate until set.

YIELD: 6-8 SERVINGS.

cinnamon apple tartlets

PREP/TOTAL TIME: 15 MIN.

These flaky, sweet treats are a fun ending to a great weeknight meal. And they come together in just under fifteen minutes.

Taste of Home Test Kitchen

1 tube (8 ounces) refrigerated crescent rolls
4-1/2 teaspoons cinnamon-sugar, divided
1 large tart apple, thinly sliced

1 Separate crescent dough into four rectangles; place on an ungreased baking sheet. Seal perforations. Sprinkle with 3 teaspoons cinnamon-sugar.

2 Bake at 375° for 5 minutes. Arrange the apple slices over the dough; sprinkle with the remaining cinnamon-sugar. Bake 5-8 minutes longer or until golden brown. Serve warm.

YIELD: 4 SERVINGS.

frozen chocolate mint dessert

PREP/TOTAL TIME: 30 MIN. + FREEZING

- 1 package fudge brownie mix (13-inch x 9-inch pan size)
- 2 egg whites
- 1/4 cup unsweetened applesauce
- 2 teaspoons vanilla extract
- 1/2 cup baking cocoa
- 1-1/2 cups fat-free milk
- 2 packages (16 ounces each) large marshmallows
- 1/2 teaspoon mint extract
- 1 carton (16 ounces) frozen reduced-fat whipped topping, thawed
- 2/3 cup cream-filled chocolate sandwich cookie crumbs

1 In a large bowl, combine the brownie mix, egg whites, applesauce and vanilla. Spread into a 13-in. x 9-in. baking dish coated with cooking spray. Bake at 350° for 18-22 minutes or until a toothpick inserted near the center comes out clean. Cool on a wire rack.

2 In a Dutch oven, combine cocoa and milk. Cook and stir over medium heat until cocoa is dissolved. Stir in marshmallows until melted. Remove from the heat; stir in extract. Cool completely.

3 Fold in whipped topping. Spread over brownies. Sprinkle with cookie crumbs. Cover and freeze for at least 8 hours. Remove from the freezer 10 minutes before serving.

YIELD: 24 SERVINGS.

A fusion of late-summer fruits, these crisps make a simple dessert—and what's left can be kept for breakfast. Look for apple crisp mix in the produce department of your grocery store.

Nicole Werner
Cleveland, OH

nectarine plum crisps

PREP: 20 MIN. BAKE: 20 MIN.

1 package (9 ounces) apple crisp mix
6 tablespoons cold butter
2 cups sliced fresh nectarines
2 cups sliced fresh plums
2 teaspoons cornstarch
Vanilla ice cream, optional

1 Place crisp mix in a small bowl; cut in butter until mixture resembles coarse crumbs. Spoon half of the mixture into four 10-oz. ramekins or custard cups coated with cooking spray; set remaining crumb mixture aside.

2 In another bowl, combine the nectarines, plums and cornstarch. Spoon into prepared dishes. Sprinkle with reserved crumb mixture. Bake at 375° for 20-23 minutes or until filling is bubbly and topping is golden. Serve warm with ice cream if desired.

YIELD: 4 SERVINGS.

cranberry cream pie

PREP: 15 MIN. BAKE: 35 MIN. + CHILLING

2-1/2 cups whole-berry cranberry sauce
1 pastry shell (9 inches), baked
1 package (8 ounces) cream cheese, softened
2/3 cup sugar
2 eggs, lightly beaten
3 tablespoons all-purpose flour
1 teaspoon vanilla extract

1 Spread the cranberry sauce over the bottom of pastry shell. In a small bowl, beat the cream cheese and sugar until smooth. Beat in the eggs, flour and vanilla on low speed just until combined. Pour over the cranberry layer.

2 Bake at 350° for 35-40 minutes or until center is set. Cool on a wire rack. Cover and refrigerate for at least 4 hours before cutting.

YIELD: 8 SERVINGS.

fruit pizza

PREP/TOTAL TIME: 30 MIN. + CHILLING

1 tube (16-1/2 ounces) refrigerated sugar
   cookie dough

1 cup sugar, divided

2 tablespoons cornstarch

1/2 cup orange juice

1/4 cup lemon juice

1 package (8 ounces) cream cheese, softened

1 tablespoon milk

1 teaspoon grated orange peel

2/3 cup heavy whipping cream

1-1/2 cups halved fresh strawberries

1 medium peach, thinly sliced

1 small banana, sliced

1 small apple, thinly sliced

1/2 cup fresh blueberries

1 Let the dough stand at room temperature for
5-10 minutes to soften. Press onto an ungreased
14-in. pizza pan. Bake at 350° for 15-18 minutes or
until deep golden brown. Cool on a wire rack.

2 In a small saucepan, combine 1/2 cup sugar,
cornstarch and juices. Bring to a boil; cook and
stir for 2 minutes or until thickened. Remove
from the heat; set aside to cool.

3 In a large bowl, beat the cream cheese, milk,
orange peel and remaining sugar until blended.

4 In a small bowl, beat cream until soft peaks form;
fold into cream cheese mixture. Spread over crust.
Arrange fruit over filling; spread with reserved
glaze. Refrigerate until chilled.

YIELD: 12 SERVINGS.

ice cream sandwich cake

PREP/TOTAL TIME: 20 MIN. + FREEZING

19 ice cream sandwiches
1 jar (16 ounces) hot fudge ice cream topping
1-1/2 cups salted peanuts
3 Heath candy bars (1.4 ounces each)
1 carton (8 ounces) frozen whipped topping, thawed

1 Cut one ice cream sandwich in half. Place one whole and one half sandwich along a short side of an ungreased 13-in. x 9-in. dish. Arrange eight sandwiches in opposite direction in the dish. Remove lid from fudge topping. Microwave 15-30 seconds to warm; stir. Spread one-half of fudge topping over ice cream sandwiches.

2 In a food processor, combine peanuts and candy bars. Cover and pulse until chopped. Sprinkle one-half of mixture over fudge layer. Repeat layer of ice cream sandwiches and fudge topping. Spread whipped topping over top of cake. Sprinkle with remaining peanut mixture.

3 Cover and freeze for up to 2 months. Remove from the freezer 20 minutes before serving. Cut into squares.

YIELD: 15 SERVINGS.

My husband says this is the best lemon cake he's ever eaten. A cake mix and lemon gelatin make it a breeze to prepare. I like to take it to potlucks and picnics, where it always disappears quickly!

Brenda Daughtery
Lake City, FL

lemony cake

PREP: 15 MIN. BAKE: 40 MIN. + COOLING

1 package (18-1/4 ounces) yellow cake mix
1 package (3.4 ounces) lemon gelatin
4 eggs
2/3 cup water
2/3 cup canola oil
GLAZE:
1 cup confectioners' sugar
3 tablespoons lemon juice
1 teaspoon grated lemon peel

1 In a large bowl, combine the cake mix, gelatin, eggs, water and oil. Beat on low speed for 1 minute. Beat on medium for 2 minutes.

2 Pour into a greased and floured 10-in. fluted tube pan. Bake at 350° for 38-42 minutes or until a toothpick inserted near the center comes out clean. Cool for 10 minutes before removing from pan to a wire rack.

3 Combine glaze ingredients; drizzle over warm cake. Cool completely before cutting.

YIELD: 12 SERVINGS.

mocha cream torte

PREP: 30 MIN. BAKE: 20 MIN. + COOLING

1-1/2 cups graham cracker crumbs
3/4 cup packed brown sugar
1/2 cup butter, melted
1/2 cup chopped walnuts
1 tablespoon mocha-flavored coffee drink mix
1 package (18-1/4 ounces) dark chocolate cake mix

FROSTING:

1 package (8 ounces) cream cheese, softened
2 tablespoons butter, softened
2 tablespoons sour cream
3 tablespoons mocha-flavored coffee drink mix
4 cups confectioners' sugar

1 Grease and flour three 9-in. round baking pans. Line bottoms with waxed paper; grease and flour the paper. In a small bowl, combine the cracker crumbs, brown sugar, butter, walnuts and drink mix; press into prepared pans.

2 Prepare cake batter according to package directions; pour over prepared crusts. Bake according to package directions. Cool for 10 minutes; remove from pans to wire racks to cool completely. Remove waxed paper.

3 For frosting, in a large bowl, beat the cream cheese, butter, sour cream and drink mix until fluffy. Add confectioners' sugar; beat until smooth. Place one cake layer, crunchy side up, on a serving plate. Spread with 3/4 cup frosting. Repeat with remaining layers and frosting. Store in the refrigerator.

YIELD: 12-16 SERVINGS.

EDITOR'S NOTE: This recipe was tested with Pillsbury dark chocolate cake mix.

black forest cake

PREP: 10 MIN. BAKE: 25 MIN. + CHILLING

1 package (9 ounces) chocolate cake mix
1/2 cup water
1 egg
1 package (3 ounces) cream cheese, softened
2 tablespoons sugar
1 carton (8 ounces) frozen whipped topping, thawed
1 can (21 ounces) cherry pie filling

1 In a small bowl, beat the cake mix, water and egg on medium speed for 3-4 minutes. Pour into a greased 9-in. springform pan; place pan on a baking sheet.

2 Bake at 350° for 23-25 minutes or until cake springs back when lightly touched. Cool on a wire rack.

3 In a small bowl, beat cream cheese and sugar until fluffy; fold in whipped topping. Spread pie filling over cake; top with cream cheese mixture. Cover and refrigerate for 4 hours. Remove sides of pan.

YIELD: 6-8 SERVINGS.

Whether celebrating the holidays or hosting a fabulous get-together, creating fun and festive food is easy with these quick-to-fix recipes.

holidays & parties

You can make this dessert seasonal by changing what you "plant" in the cookie pudding. For a harvest party, replace the strawberry rose garnish with mini candy pumpkins. Kids love finding the gummy worms in the cute pots.

Christine Panzarella
Buena Park, CA

cookie pudding pots

PREP/TOTAL TIME: 15 MIN.

6 new terra-cotta flowerpots (3-1/2-inch diameter)

4 cups cold whole milk

2 packages (3.9 ounces each) instant chocolate fudge pudding mix

7 cream-filled chocolate sandwich cookies, crushed, divided

6 medium fresh strawberries

12 mint sprigs

1 Line flowerpots with plastic wrap; set aside. In a large bowl, whisk the milk and pudding mixes for 2 minutes. Let stand for 2 minutes or until soft-set.

2 Sprinkle 2 teaspoons of cookie crumbs into each flowerpot. Top each with 2/3 cup pudding; sprinkle with remaining crumbs. Cut each strawberry to resemble a rose.

3 Garnish each pot with a strawberry rose and mint sprigs. Refrigerate until serving.

YIELD: 6 SERVINGS.

ham with
ruby-red glaze

PREP: 5 MIN. BAKE: 2 HOURS + STANDING

  1 boneless fully cooked ham (about 4 pounds)
  3/4 cup packed brown sugar
  3/4 cup creamy French salad dressing

1 Place the ham on a rack in a shallow roasting pan.
  Cover and bake at 325° for 1-1/2 hours.

2 In a small microwave-safe bowl, combine the brown
  sugar and salad dressing. Cover and microwave on
  high for 30-60 seconds or until sugar is dissolved.
  Pour 1/4 cup over the ham.

3 Bake the ham, uncovered, 30-40 minutes longer or
  until a meat thermometer reads 140°. Let the ham
  stand for 10 minutes before slicing. Serve with the
  remaining glaze.

YIELD: 12-16 SERVINGS.

almond
strawberry salad

PREP/TOTAL TIME: 10 MIN.

Everyone loves this pretty salad that's topped with strawberries
and sliced almonds. With just a few basic ingredients, it's loaded
with flavor.

Renae Rossow • Union, KY

  3 cups fresh baby spinach
  1/2 cup sliced fresh strawberries
  1/4 cup sliced honey-roasted almonds
  1 tablespoon cider vinegar
  1 tablespoon honey
  1-1/2 teaspoons sugar

1 In a large bowl, combine the spinach, strawberries
  and almonds. In a jar with a tight-fitting lid,
  combine the vinegar, honey and sugar; shake well.
  Drizzle over salad and toss to coat.

YIELD: 4 SERVINGS.

seafood en croute

PREP: 25 MIN. BAKE: 20 MIN.

- 1 package (17.3 ounces) frozen puff pastry, thawed
- 4 salmon fillets (6 ounces each)
- 1/2 pound fresh sea or bay scallops, finely chopped
- 1/3 cup heavy whipping cream
- 2 green onions, chopped
- 1 tablespoon minced fresh parsley
- 1/2 teaspoon minced fresh dill
- 1/4 teaspoon salt
- 1/8 teaspoon pepper
- 1 egg white
- 1 egg, lightly beaten

1 On a lightly floured surface, roll each pastry sheet into a 12-in. x 10-in. rectangle. Cut each sheet into four 6-in. x 5-in. rectangles. Place a salmon fillet in the center of four rectangles.

2 In a small bowl, combine the scallops, cream, onions, parsley, dill, salt and pepper. In a small bowl, beat egg white on medium speed until soft peaks form; fold into scallop mixture. Spoon about 1/2 cup over each salmon fillet.

3 Top each with a pastry rectangle and crimp to seal. With a small sharp knife, cut several slits in the top. Place in a greased 15-in. x 10-in. x 1-in. baking pan; brush with egg. Bake at 400° for 20-25 minutes or until a thermometer reads 160°.

YIELD: 4 SERVINGS.

cookie pops

PREP/TOTAL TIME: 30 MIN.

1/4 cup creamy peanut butter

20 vanilla wafers

10 Popsicle sticks

4 ounces milk chocolate candy coating, chopped

1 teaspoon shortening

M&M's miniature baking bits, optional

1 Spread peanut butter over the flat side of 10 vanilla wafers, about 1 teaspoon on each. Top each with a Popsicle stick and another vanilla wafer. Place on a waxed paper-lined baking sheet; freeze for 7 minutes.

2 In a small microwave-safe bowl, melt candy coating and shortening; stir until smooth. Dip cookie pops into chocolate, allowing excess to drip off. Return to baking sheet.

3 Decorate with baking bits if desired. Freeze for 5-6 minutes or until chocolate is set. Store in an airtight container at room temperature.

YIELD: 10 SERVINGS.

party favors

Cookie Pops make wonderful party favors for attendees of a children's get-together. Just wrap plastic wrap or a cellophane bag around each cookie pop and tie with colored ribbon. They look and taste great!

These are a cinch to bake and even more fun to decorate! We turned out happy cupcake faces, but you can top them any way that you want.

Taste of Home
Test Kitchen

fun party cupcakes

PREP: 15 MIN. BAKE: 20 MIN.

1 package (18-1/4 ounces) cake mix of
   your choice
1 can (16 ounces) vanilla frosting
Gel food coloring, optional
Assorted candies of your choice: gummy
   worms, Tic Tacs, Life Savers, red string licorice,
   Tart'n'Tinys and Chuckles

1 Prepare cake batter according to package
  directions. Fill greased or paper-lined muffin cups
  two-thirds full. Bake at 350° for 18-24 minutes
  or until a toothpick comes out clean. Cool for
  5 minutes before removing from pans to wire
  racks to cool completely.

2 Tint the frosting with food coloring if desired.
  Frost the cupcakes and decorate as desired.

YIELD: 2 DOZEN.

icy lemonade

PREP/TOTAL TIME: 5 MIN.

A blender speeds the preparation of this refreshing drink.
Lemon-lime soda adds sparkle to this light, lemony beverage.

Beth Stephas • Eagle Grove, IA

1 can (12 ounces) frozen lemonade concentrate
30 to 35 ice cubes
4 cups lemon-lime soda, chilled

1 Place half of the lemonade concentrate and 15-17
  ice cubes in a blender; add 2 cups soda. Cover and
  process on high until ice is crushed. Repeat. Serve
  in chilled glasses. Serve immediately.

YIELD: 10 CUPS.

Who can resist creamy ice cream between homemade sugar cookies? These cheerful sweets might be the perfect way to celebrate a winter get-away vacation to the beach. Or use whatever cutters suit the occasion.

Pattie Ann Forssberg
Logan, KS

beach ball ice cream sandwiches

PREP/TOTAL TIME: 35 MIN. + FREEZING

3 tablespoons butter, softened

1-1/2 cups confectioners' sugar

1/2 teaspoon vanilla extract

1 to 2 tablespoons whole milk

Red, blue, yellow and green food coloring

48 round sugar cookies

1 quart vanilla ice cream, softened

1 In a small bowl, combine the butter, confectioners' sugar, vanilla and enough milk to achieve spreading consistency. Divide frosting among five bowls; tint each a different color with red, blue, yellow and green food coloring. Leave one plain.

2 Frost tops of 24 sugar cookies with colored frostings to resemble beach balls. Let dry completely.

3 Spoon ice cream onto bottom of plain cookies; top with frosted cookies. Place in individual plastic bags; seal. Freeze until serving.

YIELD: 2 DOZEN.

I season New York strip steaks with a Caesar dressing mixture, then grill them for a tasty entree that's ready in minutes. As a side dish, I serve baked potatoes topped with chunky salsa and sour cream.

Melissa Morton
Philadelphia, PA

caesar new york strips

PREP/TOTAL TIME: 20 MIN.

4 tablespoons creamy Caesar salad dressing, divided
2 teaspoons garlic powder
1 teaspoon salt
1 teaspoon coarsely ground pepper
2 boneless beef top loin steaks (12 ounces each)

1 In a small bowl, combine 2 tablespoons salad dressing, garlic powder, salt and pepper. Spoon over both sides of steaks.

2 Grill the steaks, covered, over medium heat or broil 4 in. from the heat for 7-9 minutes on each side or until the meat reaches desired doneness (for medium-rare, a meat thermometer should read 145°; medium, 160°; well-done, 170°), basting the meat occasionally with the remaining salad dressing. When cooked to desired doneness, allow the steaks to rest, covered, for a few minutes. Cut the steaks in half to serve.

YIELD: 4 SERVINGS.

steak primer
Top loin steak may be labeled as strip steak, Kansas City steak, ambassador steak, New York strip steak or boneless club steak depending upon your region.

stars and stripes forever dessert

PREP: 30 MIN. BAKE: 10 MIN. + COOLING

1 sheet frozen puff pastry, thawed
1 to 2 tablespoons water
1 tablespoon coarse sugar
2 cups sliced fresh strawberries
1-1/2 cups fresh raspberries
1 cup fresh blueberries
1/4 cup plus 1 tablespoon sugar, divided
1/2 cup heavy whipping cream
1 cup (8 ounces) sour cream

1 On a lightly floured surface, roll out the pastry to 1/8-in. thickness. Cut with floured star-shaped cookie cutters. Place 1 in. apart on parchment paper-lined baking sheets. Bake at 400° for 8-10 minutes or until golden brown. Remove to wire racks. Brush lightly with water and sprinkle with coarse sugar. Cool.

2 In a large bowl, combine berries and 1/4 cup sugar; set aside. In a small bowl, beat cream until it begins to thicken. Add remaining sugar; beat until soft peaks form. Place sour cream in a small serving bowl; fold in whipped cream.

3 Place bowl on a serving platter. Spoon berry mixture onto platter; top with pastry stars.

YIELD: 8 SERVINGS.

pumpkin gingerbread trifle

PREP/TOTAL TIME: 40 MIN. + CHILLING

2 packages (14-1/2 ounces each) gingerbread cake mix

1 package (4.6 ounces) cook-and-serve vanilla pudding mix

3 cups whole milk

1 can (29 ounces) solid-pack pumpkin

1/2 cup packed brown sugar

1 carton (12 ounces) frozen whipped topping, thawed, divided

1 Prepare and bake gingerbread according to package directions, using two greased 9-in. round baking pans. Cool completely on wire racks.

2 Meanwhile, for pudding, in a large saucepan, combine pudding mix and milk; stir until smooth. Cook and stir over medium heat until mixture comes to a boil. Cook and stir 1-2 minutes longer or until thickened. Remove from the heat; cool to room temperature. Combine pumpkin and brown sugar; stir into pudding.

3 In a 4-qt. glass serving bowl, crumble one gingerbread cake; gently press down. Top with half of pudding mixture and whipped topping. Repeat layers. Cover and refrigerate overnight.

YIELD: 25 SERVINGS (1 CUP EACH).

Cake mix gives these chocolate sandwich cookies a head start. You can even have kids help assemble the "spiders!"

Nella Parker
Hersey, MI

creepy spiders

PREP: 30 MIN. BAKE: 10 MIN.

1 package (18-1/4 ounces) chocolate fudge cake mix

1/2 cup butter, melted

1 egg

1 can (16 ounces) chocolate frosting

Shoestring black licorice, cut into 1-1/2 inch pieces

1/4 cup red-hot candies

1 In a large bowl, combine the cake mix, butter and egg (dough will be stiff). Shape into 1-in. balls.

2 Place 2 in. apart on ungreased baking sheets. Bake at 350° for 10-12 minutes or until set. Cool for 1 minute before removing from pans to wire racks.

3 Spread a heaping teaspoonful of frosting over the bottom of half of the cookies. Place four licorice pieces on each side of cookies for spider legs; top with remaining cookies. For eyes, use frosting to attach two red-hot candies to top of each spider.

YIELD: ABOUT 2 DOZEN.

magic wands

PREP: 50 MIN. COOK: 5 MIN. + STANDING

1-1/2 cups white baking chips
1 package (10 ounces) pretzel rods
Colored candy stars or sprinkles
Colored sugar or edible glitter

1 In a microwave, melt chips; stir until smooth. Dip each pretzel rod halfway into melted chips; allow excess to drip off. Sprinkle with candy stars and colored sugar. Place on a wire rack for 15 minutes or until set. Store in an airtight container.

YIELD: 2 DOZEN.

EDITOR'S NOTE: Edible glitter is available from Wilton Industries. Call 1-800/794-5866 or visit www.wilton.com.

pumpkin cheese ball

PREP/TOTAL TIME: 20 MIN. + CHILLING

1 package (8 ounces) cream cheese, softened

1 carton (8 ounces) spreadable chive and onion cream cheese

2 cups (8 ounces) shredded sharp cheddar cheese

2 teaspoons paprika

1/2 teaspoon cayenne pepper

1 celery rib or broccoli stalk

Sliced apples and assorted crackers

1 In a small bowl, beat cream cheeses until smooth. Stir in the cheddar cheese, paprika and cayenne. Shape into a ball; wrap in plastic wrap. Refrigerate for 4 hours or until firm.

2 With a knife, add vertical lines to the cheese ball to resemble a pumpkin; insert a celery rib or broccoli stalk for the stem. Serve with apples and crackers.

YIELD: 2-1/2 CUPS.

caramel pumpkin dip

PREP/TOTAL TIME: 10 MIN.

Served with vanilla wafers, graham cracker sticks or even apple slices, this cool, rich dip from our home economists makes a special autumn snack.

Taste of Home Test Kitchen

4 ounces cream cheese, softened

1/2 cup confectioners' sugar

1/2 cup canned pumpkin

1/3 cup caramel ice cream topping

1/4 cup sour cream

1/2 teaspoon ground cinnamon

1/4 teaspoon ground nutmeg

Vanilla wafers or graham cracker sticks

1 In a small bowl, beat cream cheese and confectioners' sugar until smooth. Gradually add the pumpkin, caramel topping, sour cream, cinnamon and nutmeg, beating until smooth. Serve with vanilla wafers or graham cracker sticks. Refrigerate leftovers.

YIELD: 2-1/2 CUPS.

butterscotch bubble bread

PREP: 25 MIN. + RISING BAKE: 20 MIN.

16 maraschino cherries, drained and patted dry

1/3 cup chopped nuts

1/3 cup flaked coconut

1 loaf (1 pound) frozen bread dough, thawed and cut into 24 pieces

1 package (3-1/2 ounces) cook-and-serve butterscotch pudding mix

1/4 cup packed brown sugar

1/2 teaspoon ground cinnamon

6 tablespoons butter, melted

1 Arrange cherries on the bottom of a greased 10-in. fluted tube pan. Sprinkle with nuts and coconut. Arrange dough pieces over coconut.

2 Combine the dry pudding mix, brown sugar and cinnamon; sprinkle over dough. Drizzle with butter. Cover and let rise in a warm place until doubled, about 1-1/2 hours.

3 Bake at 375° for 20-25 minutes or until golden brown. Cool for 5 minutes before inverting onto a serving plate. Serve warm.

YIELD: 12-14 SERVINGS.

We dreamed up this combination for a yummy treat to take into school before our Thanksgiving break. They celebrate the season and are great for kids. Everyone loved them!

Megan and
Mitchell Vogel
Jefferson, WI

pilgrim hat cookies

PREP/TOTAL TIME: 1 HOUR

1 cup vanilla frosting

7 drops yellow food coloring

32 miniature peanut butter cups

1 package (11-1/2 ounces) fudge-striped cookies

32 pieces orange mini Chiclets gum

1 In a small shallow bowl, combine frosting and food coloring. Remove paper liners from peanut butter cups.

2 Holding the bottom of a peanut butter cup, dip top of cup in yellow frosting. Position over center hole on the bottom of cookie, forming the hatband and crown. Add a buckle of Chiclets gum. Repeat with remaining cups and cookies.

YIELD: 32 COOKIES.

treats in tow

Be sure to allow the icing on these cookies to completely dry before storing them. To store or transport the cookies, layer them in a container (with a lid), and separate each layer with waxed paper, then cover.

cranberry gelatin squares

PREP/TOTAL TIME: 30 MIN. + CHILLING

2 cans (8 ounces each) crushed pineapple

2 packages (3 ounces each) strawberry gelatin

3/4 cup cold water

1 can (14 ounces) jellied cranberry sauce

1/3 cup chopped pecans

1 tablespoon butter

1/2 cup cold whole milk

1/2 cup heavy whipping cream

1 package (3.4 ounces) instant vanilla pudding mix

1 package (3 ounces) cream cheese, softened

1 Drain pineapple, reserving juice in a 1-cup measuring cup. Add enough water to measure 1 cup. Set pineapple aside.

2 In a small saucepan over medium heat, bring pineapple juice mixture to a boil. Remove from the heat; stir in gelatin until dissolved. Stir in cold water; transfer to a bowl. Cover and refrigerate until partially set.

3 In a small bowl, combine cranberry sauce and reserved pineapple; stir into gelatin mixture. Pour into a 9-in. square dish; cover and refrigerate until firm.

4 Place pecans and butter in a shallow baking pan. Bake at 350° for 8 minutes or until golden brown, stirring occasionally; cool.

5 In a small bowl, whisk the milk, cream and pudding mix for 2 minutes. Let stand for 2 minutes or until soft-set.

6 In a small bowl, beat cream cheese until smooth. Add pudding mixture; beat on low speed just until combined. Spread over gelatin. Sprinkle with toasted pecans. Chill until firm.

YIELD: 12 SERVINGS.

My family always requests this turkey at family gatherings. The Italian dressing adds zip and moistness that you don't find in other recipes. If you'd like, you can make a flavorful gravy from the pan drippings.

Cindy Carlson
Ingleside, TX

moist turkey breast

PREP: 10 MIN. BAKE: 2 HOURS + STANDING

1 bone-in turkey breast (about 7 pounds)
1 teaspoon garlic powder
1/2 teaspoon onion powder
1/2 teaspoon salt
1/4 teaspoon pepper
1-1/2 cups Italian salad dressing

1 Place turkey breast in a greased 13-in. x 9-in. baking dish. Combine the seasonings; sprinkle over turkey. Pour dressing over the top.

2 Cover and bake at 325° for 2 to 2-1/2 hours or until a meat thermometer reads 170°, basting occasionally with the pan drippings. Let stand for 10 minutes before slicing.

YIELD: 12-14 SERVINGS.

baked onion dip

PREP: 5 MIN. BAKE: 40 MIN.

Some people like this cheesy dip so much that they can't tear themselves away from the appetizer table to eat their dinner.

Mona Zignego • Hartford, WI

1 cup mayonnaise
1 cup chopped sweet onion
1 tablespoon grated Parmesan cheese
1/4 teaspoon garlic salt
1 cup (4 ounces) shredded Swiss cheese
Minced fresh parsley, optional
Assorted crackers

1 In a bowl, combine mayonnaise, onion, Parmesan cheese and garlic salt; stir in Swiss cheese. Spoon into a 1-qt. baking dish.

2 Bake, uncovered, at 325° for 40 minutes. Sprinkle with parsley if desired. Serve with crackers.

YIELD: 2 CUPS.

cranberry ham loaf

PREP: 20 MIN. BAKE: 70 MIN.

1 egg, lightly beaten

1 cup whole milk

2 medium onions, chopped

1 medium green pepper, chopped

1 cup soft bread crumbs

1-1/2 pounds ground fully cooked ham

1 pound bulk pork sausage

1 can (14 ounces) whole-berry cranberry sauce

1/4 cup water

1 tablespoon light corn syrup

1 In a large bowl, combine the egg, milk, onions, green pepper and bread crumbs. Crumble ham and sausage over mixture and mix well.

2 Pat into an ungreased 9-in. x 5-in. loaf pan (pan will be full). Place on a baking sheet. Bake, uncovered, at 350° for 70-80 minutes or until a meat thermometer reads 160°.

3 In a small saucepan, combine the cranberry sauce, water and corn syrup. Bring to a boil. Reduce heat; simmer, uncovered, for 5 minutes or until thickened. Remove ham loaf to a serving platter; serve with cranberry sauce.

YIELD: 8 SERVINGS.

spiced mixed fruit

PREP: 15 MIN. BAKE: 50 MIN.

2 packages (8 ounces each) mixed dried fruit
1 can (15 ounces) fruit cocktail, undrained
1 cup raisins
1 cup apple cider or juice
1/2 cup brandy or additional apple cider or juice
4-1/2 teaspoons chopped crystallized ginger
1-1/2 teaspoons ground cardamom
1-1/2 teaspoons ground allspice
2 medium apples, chopped
1 cup fresh or frozen cranberries

1 In a 3-qt. baking dish, combine the first eight ingredients. Cover and bake at 350° for 35-40 minutes or until fruit is softened.

2 Stir in apples and cranberries. Bake, uncovered, for 15-20 minutes or until apples are tender. Serve warm or at room temperature.

YIELD: 6-1/2 CUPS.

holiday sandwich cookies

PREP/TOTAL TIME: 20 MIN.

6 ounces white or milk chocolate candy coating, coarsely chopped

50 to 55 cream-filled chocolate sandwich cookies

Christmas-shaped sprinkles, snowflake decors and red and green sprinkles

1 In a microwave, melt 2 oz. of candy coating at a time, stirring until smooth. Spread over cookie tops; decorate immediately. Place on waxed paper until set. Repeat with remaining cookies.

YIELD: 50-55 COOKIES.

edible gifts

For an easy, quick Christmas gift, stack cookies in a wide-mouth canning jar, cover the lid with fabric and screw on the band. You may also want to include the recipe for the cookies.

individual beef wellingtons

PREP: 30 MIN. BAKE: 25 MIN.

6 beef tenderloin steaks (1-1/2 to 2 inches thick and 8 ounces each)

4 tablespoons butter, divided

3 sheets frozen puff pastry, thawed

1 egg, lightly beaten

1/2 pound sliced fresh mushrooms

1/4 cup chopped shallots

2 tablespoons all-purpose flour

1 can (10-1/2 ounces) condensed beef consomme, undiluted

3 tablespoons port wine

2 teaspoons minced fresh thyme

1 In a large skillet, brown steaks in 2 tablespoons butter for 2-3 minutes on each side. Remove and keep warm.

2 On a lightly floured surface, roll each puff pastry sheet into a 14-in. x 9-1/2-in. rectangle. Cut into two 7-in. squares (discard scraps). Place a steak in the center of each square. Lightly brush pastry edges with water. Bring opposite corners of pastry over steak; pinch seams to seal tightly. Cut four small slits in top of pastry.

3 Place in a greased 15-in. x 10-in. x 1-in. baking pan. Brush with egg. Bake at 400° for 25-30 minutes or until pastry is golden brown and meat reaches desired doneness (for medium-rare, a meat thermometer should read 145°; medium, 160°; well-done, 170°).

4 Meanwhile, in the same skillet, saute mushrooms and shallots in remaining butter for 3-5 minutes or until tender. Combine flour and consomme until smooth; stir into mushroom mixture. Bring to a boil; cook and stir for 2 minutes or until thickened. Stir in wine and thyme. Cook and stir 2 minutes longer. Serve with beef.

YIELD: 6 SERVINGS.

These cookies aren't just tasty, they're adorable, too! The cookie dough is also excellent for rolling and making cut-out cookies, such as Santa Claus-shaped or Christmas tree-shaped cookies.
Taste of Home Test Kitchen

jolly snowman cookies

PREP: 1 HOUR + STANDING BAKE: 10 MIN./BATCH

1 tube (16-1/2 ounces) refrigerated peanut butter cookie dough

1/4 cup all-purpose flour

17 Popsicle sticks

1 pound white candy coating, coarsely chopped

Semisweet chocolate chips

9 candy corn, white portion removed

Miniature semisweet chocolate chips

Milk chocolate M&M's

Assorted colors of decorating gel

Assorted colors of Fruit Roll-Ups, cut into thin strips

1 In a small bowl, beat cookie dough and flour until combined. Shape dough into seventeen 1-1/4-in. balls and seventeen 3/4-in. balls. On ungreased baking sheets, place one large ball next to one small ball to form a snowman. Flatten each slightly with the bottom of a glass dipped in flour. Insert a Popsicle stick into each larger ball.

2 Bake at 350° for 10-12 minutes or until lightly browned. Cool completely before carefully removing to wire racks.

3 In a microwave-safe bowl, melt white candy coating at 70% power for 1 minute; stir. Microwave at additional 10- to 20-second intervals, stirring until smooth.

4 Dip snowmen in coating; allow excess to drip off. Place on waxed paper. Immediately position chocolate chips for eyes, candy corn for noses and miniature chocolate chips for mouths.

5 For earmuffs, place M&M's on either side of each face; connect with a strip of decorating gel. For scarves, place a strip of Fruit Roll-Up around each snowman. Let stand for 30 minutes or until set.

YIELD: 17 COOKIES.

These large, luscious cinnamon rolls are always a hit at my parent's Christmas brunch. The recipe yields two so you can keep one and give the other as a gift.

Kathy Wells
Brodhead, WI

gigantic cinnamon rolls

PREP: 20 MIN. + RISING BAKE: 20 MIN.

1/2 cup sugar

1/2 cup packed brown sugar

2 teaspoons ground cinnamon

2 loaves (1 pound each) frozen bread dough, thawed

1/2 cup butter, melted

1/2 cup chopped pecans

1-1/4 cups confectioners' sugar

6 teaspoons whole milk

1/2 teaspoon vanilla extract

1 In a shallow bowl, combine sugars and cinnamon; set aside. On a lightly floured surface, roll each loaf of dough into a 12-in. x 4-in. rectangle. Cut each rectangle lengthwise into four 1-in. strips. Roll each into an 18-in.-long rope. Dip in butter, then roll in the cinnamon-sugar mixture.

2 Coil one rope in the center of a greased 12-in. pizza pan. Add three more ropes, pinching ends together to fill one pan. Repeat with remaining ropes on a second pizza pan. Sprinkle with pecans and remaining cinnamon-sugar. Cover and let rise in a warm place until doubled, about 45 minutes.

3 Bake at 350° for 20-30 minutes or until golden brown. In a small bowl, combine the confectioners' sugar, milk and vanilla until smooth. Drizzle over warm rolls.

YIELD: 2 ROLLS (6-8 SERVINGS EACH).

peppermint angel roll

PREP: 30 MIN. BAKE: 15 MIN. + FREEZING

1 package (16 ounces) angel food cake mix

1 tablespoon confectioners' sugar

1/2 gallon peppermint ice cream, softened

1 jar (11-3/4 ounces) hot fudge ice cream topping, warmed

Crushed peppermint candies and additional confectioners' sugar, optional

1 Prepare cake batter according to package directions. Line a greased 15-in. x 10-in. x 1-in. baking pan with waxed paper and grease the paper. Spread batter evenly into pan. Bake at 350° for 15-20 minutes or until cake springs back when lightly touched.

2 Cool the cake for 5 minutes. Turn onto a kitchen towel dusted with confectioners' sugar. Gently peel the cake off the waxed paper. Roll up the cake in the towel jelly-roll style, starting with a short side. Cool completely on a wire rack.

3 Unroll the cake and spread ice cream over cake to within 1/2 in. of edges. Roll up again. Cover and freeze until firm.

4 Cut the cake into slices and drizzle with the hot fudge topping. If desired, garnish with crushed candies and dust with confectioners' sugar.

YIELD: 10 SERVINGS.

little holiday cakes

PREP: 20 MIN. BAKE: 15 MIN./BATCH + COOLING

Pastry for double-crust pie (9 inches)
1/2 cup seedless raspberry jam
1 package (18-1/4 ounces) red velvet cake mix
1 can (16 ounces) vanilla frosting
Red and green sprinkles

1 Roll pastry to 1/8-in. thickness. Cut into 2-1/2-in. circles. Press onto the bottom and 1/2 in. up the sides of greased muffin cups. Top each with 1 teaspoon of jam; set aside.

2 Prepare cake batter according to package directions; fill muffin cups three-fourths full. Bake at 350° for 14-16 minutes or until a toothpick inserted near the center comes out clean. Cool for 10 minutes before removing from pans to wire racks to cool completely. Frost with vanilla frosting and decorate with sprinkles.

YIELD: 2 DOZEN.

elegant eggnog dessert

PREP/TOTAL TIME: 30 MIN. + CHILLING

1 can (13-1/2 ounces) Pirouette cookies

1/2 cup graham cracker crumbs

1/4 cup butter, melted

2 packages (8 ounces each) cream cheese, softened

2 cups cold eggnog

1-1/3 cups cold whole milk

2 packages (3.4 ounces each) instant vanilla pudding mix

1/2 teaspoon rum extract

1/8 teaspoon ground nutmeg

1 cup heavy whipping cream

1 Cut each cookie into two 2-1/2-in. sections; set aside. Crush remaining 1-inch pieces. In a small bowl, combine the cookie crumbs, cracker crumbs and butter; press onto the bottom of a greased 9-in. springform pan.

2 In a large bowl, beat the cream cheese until smooth. Beat in the eggnog, milk, pudding mixes, extract and nutmeg until smooth. Whip cream until stiff peaks form. Fold whipped cream into pudding mixture. Spoon over crust. Cover and refrigerate for 6 hours or overnight.

3 Just before serving, remove sides of pan. Arrange reserved cookies around dessert and press gently into sides. Refrigerate leftovers.

YIELD: 12 SERVINGS.

EDITOR'S NOTE: This recipe was tested with commercially prepared eggnog. Reduced-fat eggnog is not recommended.

eggnog cream pies

PREP/TOTAL TIME: 35 MIN. + CHILLING

2 unbaked pastry shells (9 inches)

4 ounces cream cheese, softened

1/2 cup confectioners' sugar

1 teaspoon ground allspice

1 teaspoon ground nutmeg

2 cartons (one 8 ounces, one 12 ounces) frozen whipped topping, thawed, divided

3-3/4 cups cold eggnog

3 packages (3.4 ounces each) instant cheesecake or vanilla pudding mix

Additional ground nutmeg

1 Line unpricked pastry shells with a double thickness of heavy-duty foil. Bake at 450° for 8 minutes. Remove the foil and bake 5 minutes longer. Cool on wire racks.

2 In a small bowl, beat the cream cheese, confectioners' sugar, allspice and nutmeg until smooth. Fold in the 8-oz. carton of whipped topping. Spoon into crusts.

3 In a large bowl, whisk eggnog and pudding mixes for 2 minutes. Let stand for 2 minutes or until soft-set. Spread over cream cheese layer. Top with remaining whipped topping; sprinkle with additional nutmeg. Cover and refrigerate for 8 hours or overnight.

YIELD: 2 PIES (8 SERVINGS EACH).

EDITOR'S NOTE: This recipe was tested with commercially prepared eggnog.

white chocolate raspberry truffles

PREP/TOTAL TIME: 20 MIN. + CHILLING

1 package (8 ounces) cream cheese, softened
1 cup white baking chips, melted
3/4 cup crushed vanilla wafers (about 25 wafers)
1/4 cup seedless raspberry preserves
2/3 cup finely chopped almonds, toasted

1 In a small bowl, beat cream cheese until smooth. Beat in the melted chips, wafer crumbs and preserves. Cover and refrigerate for 2 hours or until easy to handle.

2 Shape into 1-in. balls; roll in almonds. Store in an airtight container in the refrigerator.

YIELD: ABOUT 3-1/2 DOZEN.

toasting nuts

Spread the nuts on a baking sheet and bake at 350° for 5 to 10 minutes or until lightly toasted. Be sure to watch them carefully so they don't burn.

I bake this scrumptious, fruit-topped layer cake every February 14 for my husband's birthday. The heart shape is really pretty for Valentine's Day, plus it's easier to make than it looks.

Amy Freitag
Stanford, IL

red velvet heart torte

PREP: 25 MIN. BAKE: 30 MIN. + COOLING

1 package (18-1/4 ounces) red velvet cake mix
1 carton (6 ounces) raspberry yogurt
1/3 cup confectioners' sugar
1 carton (12 ounces) frozen whipped topping, thawed
1 cup raspberry pie filling

1 Prepare cake batter according to package directions. Pour into two greased and floured 9-in. heart-shaped baking pans. Bake at 350° for 30-33 minutes or until a toothpick inserted near the center comes out clean. Cool for 10 minutes before removing from pans to wire racks to cool completely.

2 In a large bowl, combine yogurt and confectioners' sugar; fold in whipped topping. Cut each cake horizontally into two layers. Place bottom layer on a serving plate; top with a fourth of the yogurt mixture. Repeat layers three times. Spread pie filling over the top to within 1 in. of edges. Cover and refrigerate until serving.

YIELD: 14 SERVINGS.

EDITOR'S NOTE: This recipe was tested with Duncan Hines red velvet cake mix.

caramel

Caramel Chocolate Fondue, 191
Caramel Crackers 'n' Nuts, 13
Caramel Heavenlies, 201
Caramel Pumpkin Dip, 225
Pineapple-Caramel Sponge Cakes, 182

cheese

Baked Onion Dip, 229
Bean Soup with Cheddar
    Cornmeal Dumplings, 106
Beer Cheese Soup, 103
Breadsticks for Two, 83
Cabbage Bowl Nibbler Dip, 28
Cauliflower Au Gratin, 77
Cheddar Broccoli Quiche, 47
Cheddar Crab Bites, 27
Cheddar Skillet Corn Bread, 88
Cheese 'n' Ham Biscuit Drops, 20
Cheeseburger Soup, 113
Cheesy Pesto Bread, 83
Chili-Cheese Breakfast Bake, 49
Chili-Cheese Mashed Potatoes, 64
Colorful Mac 'n' Cheese, 161
Con Queso Spirals, 75
Eggs with Feta and Asparagus, 43
Garlic Toast Pizzas, 158
Golden Garlic Bread, 96
Ham 'n' Cheddar Corn Bread, 85
Havarti Cheese Puff, 26
Herb Cheese Bread, 92
Herbed Garlic Bread, 95
Hot Cheddar-Mushroom Spread, 14
Italian Drop Biscuits, 93
Mini Focaccia, 90
Parmesan Pretzel Rods, 10
Parmesan Sage Scones, 87
Peppy Provolone Slices, 19
Pizza Dip, 171
Pizza Fingers, 15
Ricotta Puffs, 15
Zucchini Cheddar Biscuits, 82

cheesecake & cream cheese

Caramel Pumpkin Dip, 225
Chocolate Cherry Cheesecake, 189
Cranberry Cream Pie, 206
Eggnog Cream Pies, 239
Elegant Eggnog Dessert, 238
Peach Cheese Pie, 196
Pumpkin Cheese Ball, 225
Raspberry Cheesecake Pie, 185

cherries

Butterscotch Bubble Bread, 226
Cherry Crescent Coffee Cake, 48
Cherry Pie Dessert, 202
Cherry-Stuffed Pork Chops, 120
Chocolate Cherry Cheesecake, 189
Cinnamon Cherry Rolls, 42

chicken

Bacon Chicken Skewers, 137
Broccoli Chicken Casserole, 158
Chicken a la King, 131
Chicken 'n' Broccoli Braid, 140
Chicken Broccoli Calzones, 145
Chicken Club Brunch Ring, 39
Chicken Coleslaw Wraps, 125
Chicken Noodle Delight, 122
Chicken Turnovers, 20
Chicken Wraps, 136
Guacamole Chicken Roll-Ups, 133
Italian Chicken, 174
Jalapeno Chicken Pizza, 153
Lattice Chicken Potpie, 155
Make-Ahead Chicken Bake, 151
Pear Chutney Chicken, 126
Pesto Chicken Pasta, 154
Spicy Ranch Chicken Wings, 25
Sweet 'n' Sour Curry Chicken, 165
White Chili, 112

chocolate

Candy Cookie Cups, 192
Caramel Chocolate Fondue, 191
Chocolate Biscuit Puffs, 98
Chocolate Cherry Cheesecake, 189
Chocolate-Filled Crescents, 84
Chocolate Mint Cream Cake, 195
Chocolate-Peanut Butter Cookies, 193
Cookie Pops, 217

meatballs

Mini Hot Dogs 'n' Meatballs, 169
Sweet-and-Sour Meatballs, 160

mint

Chocolate Mint Cream Cake, 195
Cookie Pudding Pots, 214
Frozen Chocolate Mint Dessert, 204
Peppermint Angel Roll, 236

muffin mix (see corn bread & muffin mix)

mushrooms

Beef Burgundy, 176
Beef Sirloin Tip Roast, 134
Biscuit Mushroom Bake, 148
Ground Beef a la King, 157
Hot Cheddar-Mushroom Spread, 14
Individual Beef Wellingtons, 233
Mushroom Barley Casserole, 66
Omelet Quesadilla, 42
Saucy Mushroom Pork Chops, 125
Sausage Mushroom Pie, 159
Shrimp Kabobs, 121
Slow-Cooked Beef Brisket, 175
Stroganoff Soup, 114

mustard

Havarti Cheese Puff, 26
Pretzel Mustard Dip, 18

nuts & peanut butter

Almond Strawberry Salad, 215
Apricot Almond Dressing, 58
Butterscotch Bubble Bread, 226
Buttery Almond Green Beans, 76
Candy Cookie Cups, 192
Caramel Crackers 'n' Nuts, 13
Caramel Heavenlies, 201
Chocolate-Peanut Butter Cookies, 193
Coconut Pecan Waffles, 44
Cookie Pops, 217
Cranberry-Nut Coffee Cake, 37
Fancy Sugar Cookie Bars, 202

Frozen Peanut Parfait Pies, 199
Granola Trail Mix, 28
Ice Cream Sandwich Cake, 208
Mushroom Barley Casserole, 66
Peach Almond Bars, 183
Peanut Butter Delights, 192
Peanut Butter S'mores Bars, 187
Peanut Lover's Pie, 200
Pilgrim Hat Cookies, 227
Pistachio Quick Bread, 99
Pumpkin Pecan Loaves, 80
Raisin Pecan Baklava, 184
White Chocolate Raspberry Truffles, 240

oatmeal mix & granola

Blueberry Oatmeal Pancakes, 38
Granola Trail Mix, 28

onions

Baked Onion Dip, 229
Flavorful Oniony Asparagus, 59
Mediterranean Frittata, 32
Onion Meat Loaf, 169
Pineapple Shrimp Kabobs, 135
Potatoes, Peas & Pearl Onions, 56
Shrimp Kabobs, 121
Slow-Cooked Beef Brisket, 175

oranges

Orange Dip for Fruit, 27
Orange Marmalade Sweet Rolls, 49

pasta, pasta sauce & pasta dinner mix

Broccoli Chicken Casserole, 158
Caesar Orzo with Asparagus, 57
Chicken Noodle Delight, 122
Colorful Mac 'n' Cheese, 161
Con Queso Spirals, 75
Creamy Tortellini, 63
Herbed Beef with Noodles, 178
Mini Hot Dogs 'n' Meatballs, 169
Pasta Beef Soup, 109
Pesto Chicken Pasta, 154
Pesto Minestrone, 117

tomatoes

Broiled Tomatoes with Artichokes, 67
Cabbage Bowl Nibbler Dip, 28
Colorful Mac 'n' Cheese, 161
Green Chili Tomato Soup, 114
Guacamole Turkey BLTs, 139
Herbed Potatoes and Veggies, 61
Italian Chicken, 174
Pasta Beef Soup, 109
Shrimp Kabobs, 121
Taco Minestrone, 110
Terrific Tomato Tart, 11
Tomato Florentine Soup, 110

turkey

Cabbage Bowl Nibbler Dip, 28
Guacamole Turkey BLTs, 139
Italian Turkey Sandwich Loaf, 130
Moist Turkey Breast, 229
Turkey Eggs Benedict, 34
Turkey Wafflewiches, 130

vegetables (also see specific kinds)

Apricot Beef Stir-Fry, 152
Beef Vegetable Soup, 166
Ground Beef a la King, 157
Herbed Potatoes and Veggies, 61
Lattice Chicken Potpie, 155
Pesto Minestrone, 117
Potatoes, Peas & Pearl Onions, 56
Skillet Lo Mein, 65

whipped topping

Cherry Pie Dessert, 202
Eggnog Cream Pies, 239
Frozen Chocolate Mint Dessert, 204
Frozen Peanut Parfait Pies, 199
Ice Cream Sandwich Cake, 208
Orange Dip for Fruit, 27
Pumpkin Gingerbread Trifle, 222
Red Velvet Heart Torte, 241
White Chocolate Dream Torte, 190

wonton wrappers

Ranch-Sausage Wonton Cups, 17

zucchini & squash

Colorful Mac 'n' Cheese, 161
Herbed Potatoes and Veggies, 61
Pesto Minestrone, 117
Zucchini Cheddar Biscuits, 82